WHERE AI MEETS EMPATHY™

COACHING THE HUMAN SIDE OF INNOVATION

BY DR. TOWANNA BURROUS

AUTHORS on MISSION

Table of Contents

Why This Book, Why Now

The email came in at 6:47 a.m. "Your AI assistant has booked three meetings, prepared two proposals, and found five priority action items for the day."

Then, at 7:15 a.m., another message: "According to the patterns in your calendar, you might be facing decision fatigue. Do you want delegation suggestions?"

The efficiency was remarkable.

The insight, unsettling.

Somewhere between grateful and overwhelmed, most leaders are discovering that AI can handle their external world with unparalleled precision and yet leave their internal world completely untouched. They have smarter calendars but still struggle with difficult conversations. They have more prescient data but feel less present to their teams. They have faster answers but fewer moments of genuine understanding.

This is the paradox of our time: as our tools become more sophisticated, our need for human wisdom becomes all the more vital.

We are living in a moment that demands more than innovation, and it requires intention.

Artificial intelligence is reshaping the way we work, lead, and live. It writes our memos, schedules our meetings, drafts our marketing plans, and curates our learning. For some, it's a productivity revolution. For others, it's a threat to creativity, culture, and connection. However, for all of us, it's real, and it's accelerating.

In this era of rapid transformation, a bold question emerges:

What does it mean to be human in a world increasingly shaped by machines?

As a coach, educator, and founder of the Institute for Coaching Innovation (ICI), I've spent the last decade preparing leaders to listen differently to themselves, to others, and to the systems within which they operate.

My doctoral research at the University of Pennsylvania Graduate School of Education explored how U.S.-based coaches delivering virtual coaching perceived the strengths, limitations, and evolving challenges of e-coaching in business contexts. The study offered a thematic analysis of their real-world insights: what helped, what hindered, and what was possible. While my dissertation did not focus on identity directly, it revealed how trust, presence, and connection are either amplified or diminished through digital platforms. Those insights became foundational to how ICI trains coaches to integrate technology without losing human depth.

What I learned changed the way I coach, teach, and lead.

It also prepared me for this moment.

The future of leadership will not be defined solely by those who master technology. It will be defined by those who can guide humanity through this era with clarity, compassion, and courage. That is the work of coaching.

Consider the infrastructure underlying your everyday life: the bridges that safely transport you over rivers, the electrical systems that light your home, the water systems that nourish your community. It is infrastructure that is mostly unseen until something fails. It is only then that we appreciate how much we rely on these well-engineered systems to work effectively, even when under stress.

Human infrastructure operates in the same way. In organizations, it's the web of relationships, communication patterns, decision-making processes, and cultural norms that holds people together, makes them productive, and enables them to bounce back from adversity. When this infrastructure is healthy, people handle change with assurance. When it's weak or ignored, even minor disruptions trigger widespread malfunctioning.

Coaching is both the inspection system and the repair process for this human infrastructure. Coaches spot stress points before they become fractures. They reinforce load-bearing connections among individuals and teams. They engineer supports that bend under pressure instead of breaking.

In the age of AI, this infrastructure is even more essential. The more routine tasks technology takes over, the more complicated the remaining work for humans is, the more interpersonal, the more demanding of emotional intelligence. The infrastructure that underpins this work—trust, communication, cultural competence, ethical judgment—cannot be outsourced to machines. It has to be deliberately constructed and persistently nurtured.

Who Is This Book For?

This book is a call to reimagine coaching not as a soft skill or executive perk, but as a strategic imperative for navigating change. In fact, coaching is fast becoming the human infrastructure of the AI era, a vital bridge between data and discernment, automation and awareness. It is a framework for those who believe that emotional intelligence, cultural awareness, and ethical inquiry are not extras; they are essentials.

- Maybe you're a leader who's struggling with how to meet demands for efficiency while your team craves human connection.
- Maybe you're a coach who's asking yourself how you remain relevant when AI is able to create even better questions than you pose.
- Perhaps you're an organizational development practitioner who's charged with introducing AI tools while ensuring psychological safety and trust.

These dilemmas are proliferating. The legacy playbooks don't tell you how to provide feedback when algorithms are monitoring performance data. Classic leadership development doesn't teach you how to create culture when half of your team works through virtual platforms augmented by AI. Classic coaching frameworks weren't built for clients who come in with AI-driven insights into their own behavioral tendencies.

This book tackles these modern leadership challenges squarely. You'll find theory, but also tools. You'll hear from pioneers, but also practitioners. And you'll encounter the ICI 5-Phase Model, a methodical process for incorporating AI tools into coaching practice without compromising human agency at any point. You will discover how to work with AI as a thinking partner, not a replacement for human judgment. You will read about frameworks for developing real relationships when technology mediates so many interactions. You will learn about methods of coaching that honor cultural identity and systemic context, even when data point toward one-size-fits-all solutions.

Above all, you will create the emotional and moral basis to lead others through technological change while safeguarding what makes us essentially human.

How to Use This Book

This book is penned both as a comprehensive guide and a practical toolkit. Each chapter is a standalone in-depth exploration of key concepts, so the book will be useful to busy practitioners needing to address specific challenges in a hurry. However, the chapters also build on each other, offering an overall framework for the integration of AI and empathy into leadership and coaching practice.

- **Part I: Foundations**

  This section sets the conceptual foundations for this work. You'll find out what separates coaching from AI and therapy, why responsiveness to culture is not a choice, and how emotional intelligence becomes even more essential in the context of technology. These chapters form the theoretical foundation for everything that comes after.

- **Part II: Human Skills for the AI Age**

  In Part II, the focus is on the development of skills that are distinctly and irreplaceably human. You will study in-depth emotional intelligence, learn to coach across cultures, and discover how to remain present in digitally mediated relationships. These chapters include assessment tools and skill-practice exercises.

- **Part III: Coaching in Practice**

  A practical guide, this section presents the ICI frameworks for integrating AI in an ethical manner. You will be exposed to actual case studies, implementation tactics, and measurement methods that trade off efficiency and humanity. These chapters offer practical models that you can map onto your situation.

- **Part IV: Looking to the Future**
  The final section of the book covers coach training, organizational readiness, and the leadership competencies of the future. These chapters allow you to build capacity for challenges not yet on the horizon while staying grounded in time-tested human values.

In each chapter, you'll find:

- Character stories that illustrate concepts through relatable workplace scenarios
- Illustrative example scenarios contrasting AI-only solutions with human-led options
- Practice labs featuring interactive activities you can complete individually or with your team
- Reflection questions connecting content to your own leadership challenges
- Architectural insights that place coaching at the center of organizational resilience infrastructure

Whether you read cover to cover or focus on specific sections, this book is designed to meet you where you are and get you ready for where you're headed.

This isn't just a book about AI. It's a book about **what we must protect, preserve, and amplify** as we embrace it.

Because when machines are getting smarter, the most powerful thing we can do is become more deeply human.

Welcome to Where AI Meets Empathy™.

Let's begin.

PART I
FOUNDATIONS

Architects research the ground before they design a skyscraper. They look at soil makeup, determine load-bearing capacity, and learn about environmental stresses the building will encounter. Only then do they design foundations that can support all that is built atop.

The same is true in building human infrastructure for the AI era. We need to lay the foundation of knowledge that will underpin all subsequent development before we delve into sophisticated frameworks or action plans.

Part I builds this required groundwork in three interrelated studies:

- *Chapter 1: AI Is Here—Now What?* begins in personal anecdote and moves toward practical wisdom. We examine what it means to lead with humanity as technology reshapes the world around us. This chapter establishes coaching as the maintenance system for human potential, introducing the infrastructure metaphor that underpins our entire approach.

- *Chapter 2: Coaching Isn't Therapy. Nor Is It AI* establishes boundaries while building bridges. We explore the distinctions that separate coaching from therapeutic intervention and artificial intelligence, positioning it as the connective tissue between human potential and technological capability. You'll discover why pattern disruption is more vital than pattern completion in enabling authentic transformation.

- *Chapter 3: Culturally Responsive Coaching in a Technological World* deals with the fact that effective infrastructure needs to consider diverse needs and settings. We discuss how cultural identity, systemic awareness, and power dynamics inform every coaching relationship, and why AI incorporation without cultural responsiveness will exacerbate current inequities rather than solve them.

Collectively, these three chapters address key questions: What is coaching's role in an AI-augmented world? How do we maintain human depth amidst technological advancement? Why is cultural responsiveness even more critical when human growth is informed by algorithms?

The foundations you establish here will dictate whether your coaching practice is going to get more relevant or more outdated as AI keeps evolving. Solid foundations bring stability in the midst of uncertainty. They offer anchor points for innovation. They guarantee that what you construct is in the service of human flourishing and not merely organizational efficacy.

As with any worthwhile infrastructure project, this foundational work demands patience and attention to detail. The ideas might appear straightforward, but they become load-bearing pillars for all that comes after. Shortchange them, and the whole edifice wobbles. Take the time to invest in them properly, and they will undergird transformation for years ahead.

The future of coaching is not in attempting to compete with AI, but in building human infrastructure that makes AI integration ethical, effective, and empowering. That infrastructure begins with understanding exactly what coaching provides that nothing else can.

Let's build these foundations together.

AI Is Here—Now What?

Sienna D'Souza had always trusted her intuition. As an Indian–American operations director at a mid-sized consulting firm, she prided herself on leading with empathy, reading the energy in the room, knowing who needed support without their saying a word. But lately, the room was Zoom, and the signals were digital.

Her firm had adopted a powerful AI-driven performance management system. The tool generated weekly behavior summaries, tone assessments, and even collaboration scores for her team. It was fast, data-rich, and unsettling.

"I feel like I'm managing dashboards, not people." She scheduled a session with her mentor coach, Kenji, to talk through what she was noticing. "The AI flagged Leo as 15% below his delivery rate, but I just talked to him yesterday. He said he was fine."

Kenji, an executive coach, sat back for a moment, giving Sienna space to exhale before he asked, "Do you think he is fine?"

Sienna paused. "That's the thing. I used to know. Now I hesitate. I don't know whether to trust my gut, or the algorithm."

"Maybe it's not either/or," Kenji offered. "What if the AI gives you signals, but your job is to interpret what they mean in real human terms? Maybe the system can tell you what's happening. But only you can find out why."

Over the next few weeks, Sienna started experimenting. When the system flagged her colleague Ayla for low collaboration scores, she didn't assign another team-building module. Instead, she scheduled a walking meeting. Ayla shared that she was feeling over-monitored and missed the spontaneous creativity of in-person work.

With that insight, Sienna adjusted how she led meetings and started protecting time for unstructured collaboration. The metrics improved, but more importantly, Ayla did too.

By the end of the quarter, Sienna had reframed her role.

She wasn't losing her touch.

She was learning a new way to lead with data as her co-pilot and empathy as her compass.

* * *

Just like Sienna, you might be conflicted between the promise of AI efficiency and the immeasurable worth of human connection in your leadership. Happily, this chapter will allow you to discover how to implement conscious adoption principles to transform AI from a barrier to a bridge, forging more robust relationships with your team while leveraging technology's power to enhance, not replace, your natural empathetic leadership abilities.

The Room Where I First Belonged

When I first entered the doctoral program at the University of Pennsylvania's Graduate School of Education, I didn't know I was about to experience something I had never felt before: true belonging. Not just inclusion, not just access, but an environment where every voice was valued and every life experience mattered. The diversity in that room, in terms of race, gender, professional background, and life journey, was deliberate. It was designed for learning. Our professors, coordinators, and peers co-created an atmosphere where intellectual curiosity and cultural humility intersected. That space wasn't just about education. It was about evolution. And it transformed me.

I came to Penn already a coach, already a trainer. But in that space, I became something more: a leader grounded in listening, shaped by difference, and driven by the power of awareness. That moment of belonging changed how I coach, teach, and lead.

It also gave birth to this book.

I've spent the last decade coaching leaders across various industries and training over 3,500 coaches worldwide. In that time, I've learned this: most leadership development fails because there's no time or space to practice. We read the books. We go to the workshops. We nod at the theories. But then we go back to work and react the way we always have.

That's why I founded the Institute for Coaching Innovation, formerly CoachDiversity Institute. Because learning without implementation is a waste of time. Coaching without self-awareness is performative. And leadership without empathy is obsolete.

Why Coaching Is the Load-Bearing Beam of Change

Consider coaching as the organizational change infrastructure foundation. Just as bridges need firm support to bear heavy loads, leaders working through AI transformation require emotional scaffolding that will bear pressure. Blueprints are provided through traditional training programs, but coaching supplies the load-bearing structures that actually sustain growth in times of change.

In the age of AI, this infrastructure is more important than ever. As technology takes care of data processing and pattern recognition, coaches are the architectural consultants who assist leaders in developing sustainable architectures for decision-making, relationship management, and moral reasoning. We design the support systems that hold humanity together when everything else speeds up.

This book is not just about artificial intelligence. It's about the intelligence we need to lead through what's coming next.

We are entering an era where AI will change everything, from how we work to how we decide, evaluate, and even relate. But technology is not the threat. The real risk is forgetting our humanity in the process. That's where empathy becomes essential.

AI doesn't feel. It doesn't reflect. It doesn't regret or reimagine. However, it can ask better pattern-based questions than humans can generate at scale, if we train it to do so.

That's our role as leaders and coaches: to guide technology with integrity, to center humanity in every innovation, and to ensure that what we build doesn't erase who we are.

Looking back, I wish someone had told me earlier that the more self-aware you are, the more powerful you become. For too long, I was modeling others' behaviors, trying to find success by copying what looked "right." But it wasn't me. It wasn't authentic. And it certainly wasn't empowering.

I want this book to do for you what Penn did for me. I want you to feel seen. To feel called. To feel ready.

Because if you're reading this, you're not just curious about AI.

You're ready to lead the human side of innovation.

AI Is Here—Now What?

The question is not "if" AI will transform your job. It already has. The question is whether you will control how it gets utilized.

Step into any workplace today, and you'll hear people having conversations they never imagined five years ago. "Should we allow the AI to generate our performance reviews?" "How do we provide feedback when the algorithm is monitoring everything?" "What do mentoring relationships look like when the AI can respond to most technical questions?"

These aren't future concerns. They're happening right now in conference rooms, coffee shops, and team meetings across every industry.

There are some leaders who react with eagerness, plunging headlong into each emerging tool and platform. Others react with resistance, holding onto what they know and understand as the world around them changes. Both of these reactions miss the critical point: adopting AI without human wisdom yields chaos, but human wisdom without tech savvy yields irrelevance.

The leaders who successfully navigate the space in between those two options understand that AI isn't something happening to them. It's something they're actively shaping through their choices, their questions, and their values.

Consider what's already changed at your work:

- Meetings that once took hours to prepare for now occur with AI-created agendas and briefings

- Performance data that was once quarterly is now predictive and real-time
- Learning and development that was once classroom-based is now personalized and adaptive
- Communication that was once primarily human-to-human now includes human-to-AI interactions daily

Each of these shifts holds out the promise of greater efficiency and understanding. Each one also presents new quandaries related to privacy, authenticity, relationships, and meaning.

The "now what" is not about choosing between human and artificial intelligence. It is about choosing integration over replacement, intention over automation, and wisdom over mere optimization.

These choices necessitate what we can refer to as "conscious adoption"—the deliberate, ethical, and fully aware use of AI tools and their effects on organizational culture and human relationships.

Deliberate adoption poses other questions:

- In what ways does the tool augment human connection instead of replacing it?
- What values are built into this AI system, and do they align with our values?
- Who benefits from this technology, and who might be harmed by it?
- How do we maintain agency and choice in an increasingly automated environment?

The answers to such questions don't start in technology textbooks or vendors' presentations. They begin in the kind of reflective conversation that coaching allows, conversations that honor both innovation and humanity, efficiency and compassion, progress and the preservation of what matters most.

This is the reason that coaching becomes more valuable, not less, as AI emerges. Someone must hold space for the human questions that arise when machines are solving the technical ones.

Someone must help leaders process through the emotional complexity of change while retaining their moral center.

Someone must ensure that optimization does not take precedence over connection.

That person is you.

Yes, you!

Regardless of whether you are a professional coach, a leader who uses coaching skills, or an organizational developer facilitating others through change, you can step into that role.

Illustrative Example

Consider Elena, a department head whose team was struggling with new AI productivity software that tracked task completion, time spent in apps, and collaboration scores. The following is how two different approaches played out:

Scenario 1: AI-Only Support

Elena was sent automated check-ins inquiring about productivity levels and tool adoption rates. Reports generated by the AI indicated declining performance and recommended efficiency training modules. When team members complained of frustration, the AI suggested stress management applications and time optimization hacks. Elena believed she was managing metrics instead of people.

Scenario 2: AI + Empathetic Coaching

Elena engaged with a coach who utilized AI-generated findings as prompts for more meaningful discussions. If data revealed productivity lags, her coach inquired about the human narrative beneath the figures. They discovered that what the data flagged as disengagement was actually a response to feeling monitored, not supported. Elena and her coach reworked the implementation process together, making room for apprehensions, setting definite boundaries around data application, and developing confidence through incremental skill development. The identical AI equipment turned into strengths instead of hindrances since the human situation dictated their application.

The difference wasn't the technology. The difference was having someone who could interpret what the data said into what it revealed about real individuals undergoing real change.

And that journey starts here.

Chapter 1 Practice Lab

Activity 1: Infrastructure Evaluation

- Spend five minutes charting your existing support systems.
- On paper, draw three columns: Technical Tools, Human Resources, and Emotional Infrastructure.
- List what you currently rely on in each area when facing a workplace challenge.
- Observe which column is most robust and which one needs to be built up.

Infrastructure Evaluation Framework

Map your current support system across three critical areas

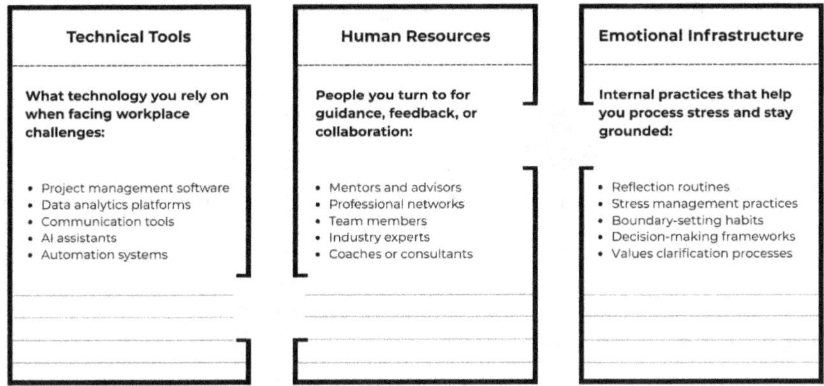

Figure 1.1 – Infrastructure Evaluation: Mapping Your Systems of Support

Activity 2: Empathy Audit

- Reflect on a recent experience of having to give tough feedback or lead change with your team.
- Note:
    - What information or data informed your strategy?
    - What human considerations did you take into account?
    - How did you achieve a balance between efficiency and connection?
- Think about how you could enhance human factors in the future.

Activity 3: Future Readiness Check

- Complete the following sentence three different ways:
    - "When AI is doing the routine work, I'd like to devote my energy to: ________"

- Notice whether your responses reflect technical capacity, relational depth, or both.
- The above reveals your intuition regarding where human value lies in an AI-enhanced workplace.

Debrief Prompt:

- What patterns did you notice across the three activities?
- What's one area of growth you want to explore further in this book?

Chapter 1 Reflection Questions

- What does "belonging" look like to you in your present work setting, and how do you think AI would alter that experience?
- When you hear the term "human infrastructure," what does it mean for your team or organization?
- How would you define "human infrastructure" in your organization, and what makes it strong or vulnerable?
- Where could technology become a catalyst for deeper trust, not just faster outcomes?
- When have you had to choose between what the data said and what your gut told you? What happened?

Moving Forward

The way forward demands courage and curiosity. AI will go on evolving whether we respond thoughtfully or act defensively. The institutions and leaders that succeed are those that approach technology as part of a broader ecosystem of human wisdom, cultural nuance, and emotional intelligence. Coaching occupies the space between what machines can calculate and what human beings need to flourish.

As we build this bridge together, we're not simply reacting to change. We're making it with intention. Chapter two investigates why coaching holds such a distinctive role in this revolution. We'll look at what distinguishes coaching from therapy and from AI, and why the distinction is more important than ever as these boundaries are blurring in practice. Your journey to empathetic leadership in the AI era begins with understanding where you stand today.

The foundation is set.

Now we build from this point.

Coaching Is Not Therapy. It's Not AI Either.

Keisha Monroe had always been the go-to leader. As a Black American woman heading operations at a national health tech company, she had built a reputation on being available, attentive, and unshakably composed. Her team consistently rated her high on engagement. She had even won the company's "People Leader of the Year" award two years ago.

But now, something felt off.

The firm had rolled out an AI-powered leadership assistant, one that analyzed calendar behavior, tone in written communications, and even micro-interactions in virtual meetings. It offered coaching suggestions, performance feedback prompts, and emotional flag alerts.

During a peer-supervision meeting with Julian, a coach colleague, she reflected, "It's like ... it sees things I don't. Last week, it flagged three of my team members as 'emotionally withdrawn.' I hadn't noticed. Then I asked one of them, and it turns out his mom was in the hospital."

Julian nodded. "It's disorienting, right? Like it's holding up a mirror, but not necessarily a truthful one."

"Exactly," Keisha said. "The tool remembers every conversation. It never has a bad day. And sometimes ... I wonder if I'm being replaced."

Julian paused. "But does it believe in your people?"

That landed.

Later that week, Keisha revisited one of the AI-generated feedback prompts: "Suggest time-tracking tools to improve focus." Instead, she scheduled one-on-one meetings, led with curiosity, and asked her team members how they were really doing.

"Honestly, I've been overwhelmed," admitted one team member. "But I didn't want to bring it up. I figured the data already said enough."

Keisha realized the system had surfaced a signal. But it was her job to turn that signal into a relationship.

By the end of the month, she wasn't competing with the AI anymore. She was translating its prompts through the lens of her own humanity.

"I see what my role is now," she later told Julian. "It doesn't know who they are."

* * *

Just as with Keisha, you may be wondering about your purpose as technology changes and asking yourself if human connection is still relevant in an age of growing automation. Fortunately, this chapter will reassure you about the invaluable uniqueness of human coaching, demystify the clear-cut differences between coaching, therapy, and AI, and demonstrate how to use technology as a tool while preserving the vital human factors that enable genuine transformation.

Where AI Ends and Human Coaching Begins

When artificial intelligence began offering answers to life's most challenging questions—"Should I leave my job?", "How do I set boundaries?", "What's my purpose?"—a predictable debate followed:

Can AI be a coach?

Some said yes. After all, AI can ask open-ended questions, offer frameworks for reflection, and even simulate empathy. Others pushed back, reminding us that coaching is not about clever questions or perfectly sequenced steps. It's about trust, presence, and deep listening.

This chapter offers a clear line in the sand: coaching is not therapy. And it's not AI. But it can sit powerfully between them, serving as the human infrastructure for leadership in an AI-augmented world.

Consider how physical infrastructure works. Roads facilitate transportation, but they also need ongoing maintenance, weather-resistant materials, and skilled engineers who understand the terrain and the load requirements. Similarly, organizational infrastructure needs people who can adapt, repair, and strengthen under pressure.

Coaching is the maintenance system for human potential. As AI sorts through information and recognizes patterns, coaches do the ongoing maintenance that allows humans to remain resilient, connected, and able to grow. They check for stress fractures before they become breakdowns. They shore up foundations when new demands test structural integrity. They make sure the entire system can deal with increased capacity without sacrificing safety.

Distinction #1: Coaching vs. Therapy

Therapy often looks to the past to heal the present. Coaching looks to the future to unlock possibilities. Both are essential. But they are not the same.

The boundary matters, especially as AI tools begin to blur them. A coaching conversation that touches on emotional patterns or identity-based struggles is not a clinical intervention. However, it is sacred work and must be approached with cultural sensitivity and care.

While transformational coaching at ICI often feels therapeutic, it is distinct from therapy in both scope and responsibility. This table clarifies how each discipline serves client growth ethically, responsibly, and in alignment with its intended role

Focus

Therapy

- "Assist me in understanding why I continuously pick demanding bosses."
- "Why do I always get nervous when presenting to senior leadership?"
- "Why do I avoid conflict, even when it's damaging to my team?"
- "I need to process why feedback triggers such strong emotional reactions in me."

Coaching

- "I'm noticing a pattern in the types of leaders I work with, and I want to unpack why I gravitate toward those who push too hard."
- "I often feel less confident around senior leaders, and I'd like to understand what's driving that and how to shift it."
- "I'm looking for ways to manage conflict that feel authentic to my leadership style."
- "I want to improve how I give and receive feedback, especially in ways that feel empowering for me and others."

Timeline

Therapy

- Examines childhood patterns that impact present relationships
- Explores how early family roles appear in workplace hierarchies
- Works to unpack experiences and resolve trauma
- The timeline is open-ended and healing-oriented

Coaching

- References the past only to inform present choices
- Focuses on current behaviors, mindset shifts, and future goals
- Offers structured, time-bound engagement

Depth

Therapy

- Addresses trauma, attachment styles, and unconscious behavior
- May include clinical diagnoses and therapeutic treatment
- Requires licensure and adherence to mental health protocols

Coaching

- Engages patterns, beliefs, and behaviors without diagnosing or treating trauma
- Acknowledges past experiences only as they inform present choices and leadership behavior
- Focuses on awareness, agency, and intentional action rather than healing or clinical intervention
- Operates within professional coaching ethics and scope of practice, not mental health licensure

When the Lines Get Blurred in Practice

The lines get blurred when:

- A client in coaching reveals that work-related stress is inducing panic attacks
- A client in therapy wishes to address career development techniques
- A leader's performance issues stem from unresolved trauma or family-of-origin patterns
- An executive's strategic thinking is obscured by depression or anxiety

In these moments, you must acknowledge the complexity without exceeding the scope of your discipline. The coach might say, "It appears that the pressure at work is affecting you in some ways that are beyond what we can address in coaching. Would it be helpful to get you linked with a therapist while we continue to work on your leadership goals?" This honors both the person's immediate needs and the coach's professional boundaries.

What Therapists Do During These Times:

Therapists facilitate emotional healing while also noting when skill-building on the practical level could use coaching assistance. Therapists, especially those familiar with coaching, may notice when a client is emotionally regulated enough to benefit from forward-looking support. The therapist could say, "Now that we've worked through the deeper emotional patterns, it may be helpful to partner with a coach who can help you take action toward your professional goals."

The Intersection Point

Both therapy and coaching are on common ground in that they are dedicated to human development, albeit from opposite directions:

Therapy: "Let's get to know what has been stopping you so that you can heal and move on."

Coaching: "Let's determine what you would like to create and help you develop the ability to obtain it."

Neither modality is superior. They serve different needs of human development, and both are useful to many people at different times of their lives, or even simultaneously, with healthy boundaries and communication between practitioners. The primary distinction remains: therapy repairs what's broken, and coaching builds what's possible. We need both for complete human flourishing.

The limits are important because they safeguard both the practitioner and the client. If a person discloses that they're triggered by those in authority, a coach may delve into current work relationships and coping mechanisms. A therapist would more likely investigate the earlier origins of that trigger and how it affects several areas of life.

Both approaches honor the person's complexity. Neither is better or worse. They serve different aspects of human development, and sometimes people need both.

Coaching and therapy can coexist with clear boundaries. Coaches are not trained to diagnose or treat emotional conditions, and therapists are not always positioned to develop forward-looking performance strategies. But when both modalities respect scope, communicate transparently, and center client well-being, they form a powerful alliance for whole-person growth.

AI can mimic coaching language, but it lacks three critical human ingredients:

- **Relational trust** – AI cannot form genuine connections or create psychological safety.
- **Cultural awareness** – AI reflects the data it was trained on, often missing lived experiences, systemic context, and nuanced identities.
- **Presence** – A coach listens beyond what is said. AI responds only to what is typed or spoken.

Even the most advanced AI tools cannot pause and say, "I sense something shifted. Would you like to stay with that?" These are what ICI calls *empathy gaps*—the spaces where simulated care cannot replace lived emotional presence. Coaching fills that gap with relational trust, cultural awareness, and intuitive listening. These aren't just human advantages. They're what makes coaching essential in the machine age.

Consider these scenarios:

- AI Response to "I'm overwhelmed":
  - "According to your calendar, you have 47 meetings this week. It is recommended by research to divide large tasks into smaller portions. Shall I create a prioritization model?"
- Coach Response to "I'm overwhelmed":
  - "I'm sensing exhaustion in your voice. Let's explore what being overwhelmed feels like for you right now before we look at your schedule."
- AI Pattern Recognition:

- "You've talked about feeling underappreciated in four of your last six journal entries. That indicates a persistent theme that we should deal with."
- Pattern Recognition Coach:
  - "I see you get excited when you talk about mentoring other people, yet your energy changes when you talk about your own progress. What do you think about that?"

The AI offers analysis. The coach offers meaning.

The AI suggests next steps. The coach holds space for the next questions. Both may be useful, but only one sits with you in the silence and helps you hear what hasn't been said.

Pattern Completion vs. Pattern Disruption

Too often, leaders come to coaching not with new questions, but with practiced answers: what sounds right, what's acceptable, and what they think others need to hear. Not that they're holding back. It's just that they've learned to finish the sentence, fill the gap, and keep the system going. Coaching breaks that up.

Where AI fills in a prompt, coaching hesitates. It breaks the cycle. It calls for a different kind of listening, one that makes room for what hasn't been said yet.

Most human interaction resembles a statistical text-prediction engine, but what matters most is when we break out of these patterns and engage in genuinely creative or deep thought.

AI excels at pattern completion. It finishes your sentences, fills your to-do list, and predicts what you'll say next. But great coaching interrupts that.

Where AI responds, coaching reflects. Where AI automates, coaching awakens. Instead of rewarding performance, coaching creates space for the things clients don't usually say out loud, even to themselves.

Coaches who interrupt predictable narratives do more than challenge the surface; they help the client encounter their assumptions in real time. That's the power of pattern disruption. While AI completes patterns based on past inputs, coaching invites clients to pause, disrupt, and choose a new response.

Here's how the difference works in practice:

Dimension	Pattern Completion (AI/Leader Habit)	Pattern Disruption (Coaching Practice)
Core Function	Predict, complete, resolve	Interrupt, pause, inquire
Typical Response Style	Predict, complete, resolve	"What am I not seeing yet?"
Driving Assumption	Predict, complete, resolve	Awareness = growth
Emotional Mode	Control, certainty	Curiosity, discomfort
AI Analogy	Auto-complete	Pattern Disruption = Gentle Interruption or Strategic Pause
Leader Example	"Here's the plan I've mapped out."	"I keep following the plan, but something feels off."
Coach's Move	Validate the pattern	Question the structure
Outcome	Repetition of known strategies	Space for new insight

This distinction is vital when you are coaching high-achieving leaders who have mastered the art of coming up with the correct answer. They arrive at coaching sessions with carefully prepared explanations and neatly worked out action plans. AI systems perpetuate this pattern of completion: the more complete and coherent the input, the more articulated the output.

Examples of Pattern Completion vs. Pattern Disruption

Coaching works differently.

An experienced coach may answer a beautifully presented challenge by saying:

"That's a good summary. Help me now to understand what you haven't told me yet."

Or:

"I can see you've got this worked out intellectually. Where are you stuck emotionally?"

Client Statement	Pattern Completion Response	Pattern Disruption Response
"I've tried three different strategies to motivate my team, and none worked."	"Maybe try combining parts of all three next time."	"What's the story you're telling yourself about why they're unmotivated?"
"I keep getting the same kind of feedback in reviews."	"Let's brainstorm ways to correct your behavior."	"What do you think people are noticing that you're not?"
"I've already decided how to handle the board meeting."	"Sounds like a solid plan."	"What part of the meeting are you not looking forward to?"
"My calendar's fully optimized, and I still feel behind."	"You could try a better time-blocking tool."	"What do you think is driving the need to optimize everything?"

Such interruptions open the possibility for genuine exploration instead of effective problem-solving.

Such invitations interrupt cognitive autopilot and invite the client to explore deeper truths. AI is built to predict. Coaching, when it's working well, interrupts.

Coaching as a Bridge

Rather than competing with AI or trying to medicalize coaching, we can embrace coaching for what it truly is: a bridge between potential and performance, presence and progress.

It is future-focused, action-oriented, and built on the radical belief that people are whole, creative, and capable even in times of uncertainty.

AI may offer insights, but only coaches can invite transformation.

This is especially true in moments when leaders are:

- Navigating racial or cultural identity in the workplace
- Wrestling with burnout, optics, or performance pressure
- Reimagining their role in a future where technology is reshaping humanity

Think of coaching as architectural engineering for human development. Any successful bridge requires some structural elements:

- Foundational pillars are rooted in bedrock principles. In coaching, these pillars are trust, presence, and cultural awareness. They must be strong enough and deep enough to support all that will be constructed on them. AI can provide information but cannot construct the relational foundation upon which change is possible.

- Load-bearing structures spread weight safely across the span. Coaching conversations build these structures by attentive listening, strategic questioning, and ongoing attention to both individual development and systemic pressures. When leaders confront accelerated change, these structures avoid collapse under heightened stress.

- Scaffolding systems offer temporary support in periods of construction. Coaches give emotional scaffolding in periods of transition, holding space for ambiguity while individuals build new competencies. This scaffolding can be modified, relocated, or made more robust as required, as opposed to many current AI structures which often deliver one-size-fits-all solutions due to the limits of their training data.

- Expansion joints permit movement without causing structural damage. Successful coaches incorporate flexibility into development plans, understanding that growth is seldom linear and that individuals require room to modify objectives as situations evolve.

The bridge itself spans two distinct locations: where a person is and where they need to go. AI can chart the landscape and plot the best courses. But coaches traverse it with individuals, compensating for weather conditions, identifying landmarks, and guaranteeing safe crossings.

These are not algorithmic moments. These are coaching moments.

Toward an Augmented Coaching Model

As we move deeper into the book, we'll explore how coaches can use AI not to replace their presence, but to enhance their practice. From journaling prompts to theme tracking to multilingual support, AI offers an incredible opportunity when used ethically and intentionally.

As we'll explore later in the ICI 5-Phase Model, coaching doesn't compete with AI. It partners with it. When integrated with consent, transparency, and cultural awareness, AI tools can enhance reflection, support accessibility, and increase insight. But it is the coach who interprets, contextualizes, and transforms.

And we must never forget:

Coaching starts and ends with the human being. Not the tool.

The Cost of Getting It Wrong

When companies substitute human coaching with AI-only alternatives, the ramifications go beyond personal growth. They hazard building cultures in which efficiency trumps empathy, in which data dictates choices without regard for human context, and in which individuals feel surveilled instead of supported.

Current workplace surveys indicate that 68% of workers feel disconnected from their managers when feedback is primarily in digital format. Employees experiencing workplace disconnectedness, the feeling of being different and distant from others in the workplace, show significantly impaired job performance and increased cognitive failures (Petitta and Ghezzi, 2023).

When people don't feel heard or seen at work, they disconnect. They leave. They withhold their best ideas.

The economic costs are significant: turnover, reduced innovation, and diminished productivity. But the human costs are deeper. People lose confidence in their own judgment when algorithms consistently second-guess their intuition. They no longer show up with their whole selves when systems only recognize limited forms of intelligence or communication styles.

Organizations that achieve a balance between AI analysis and human connection, on the other hand, report contrasting results. They experience higher trust levels, enhanced collaboration, and more durable performance gains. Individuals feel nurtured instead of monitored. They build internal capacities that benefit them for their entire careers, not only the present project.

The decision isn't AI or coaching. The decision is technological efficiency or human flourishing. The ones who opt for both will be the ones with the competitive edge.

Illustrative Example

David, a marketing manager, noticed that one of his team members, Alex, had been missing deadlines and appeared spaced out in meetings. Here is how two approaches unfolded:

Scenario 1: AI-Only Approach

David employed the firm's performance management AI to evaluate Alex's productivity metrics. The system highlighted reduced output, erratic work habits, and missed collaboration opportunities. It suggested a performance improvement plan with targeted metrics, recommended training modules on time management, and suggested bi-weekly check-ins with an emphasis on goal attainment. David arranged to discuss these suggestions with Alex in a meeting.

Scenario 2: AI + Empathetic Coaching Style

David reviewed the same AI-generated information but used it as background information, not the icebreaker. He started instead by asking how things were going overall with Alex. Through careful listening, he found out that Alex was caring for an elderly parent while managing additional responsibilities at work. The performance issues weren't about capability or commitment; they were about competing priorities and emotional exhaustion.

They discussed possibilities together: flexible scheduling, temporary reassignment of projects, and caregiver support resources. David also reminded Alex of the company's employee assistance program for personal support outside of coaching. The AI information identified the issue, but the human discussion uncovered the solution.

Alex's performance returned to normal in a month, and their participation actually increased because they felt like they were being assisted rather than monitored.

The distinction wasn't the information at hand. The distinction was the utilization of that information to initiate a human discussion instead of finishing one.

Chapter 2 Practice Lab

These exercises help you operationalize the distinctions between AI, therapy, and coaching, not as theory, but as practice.

Activity 1: Boundary Mapping

- Draw three circles on a page and title them "Therapy Space," "Coaching Space," and "AI Space."
    - Here is an example:

Professional Support Spaces

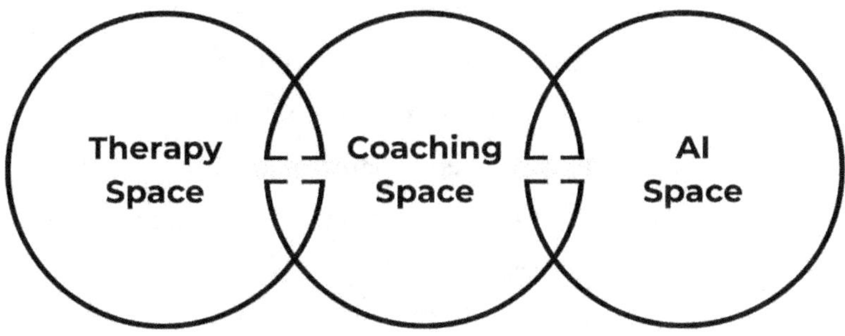

Figure 2.1 – Boundary Mapping: Defining the Edges of Professional Practice

- In each circle, write what you think belongs in that space when facilitating others' growth.
- Pay attention to where the circles would overlap and where they need to be separate.
- Reflect on how this clarity would alter your practice in facilitating team members or clients.

Activity 2: Infrastructure Evaluation

- Reflect on a recent tough conversation with a colleague or team member.

- Note:
    - What data or information you had
    - What you intuitively picked up below the surface
    - How you juggled problem-solving and presence
- Mark which aspects an AI system might have been able to provide and which needed human judgment.

Activity 3: Bridge Building Practice

- Choose someone you are coaching (as a manager, coach, or colleague) right now.
- Establish their current state and their desired state.
- Now map out the "bridge elements" they might need:
    - What groundwork of trust building do they need?
    - What scaffold support can help them through transition?
    - Where do they need expansion joints for flexibility?
    - How can you provide structure support that is tailored to their specific needs?
- Here is an example:

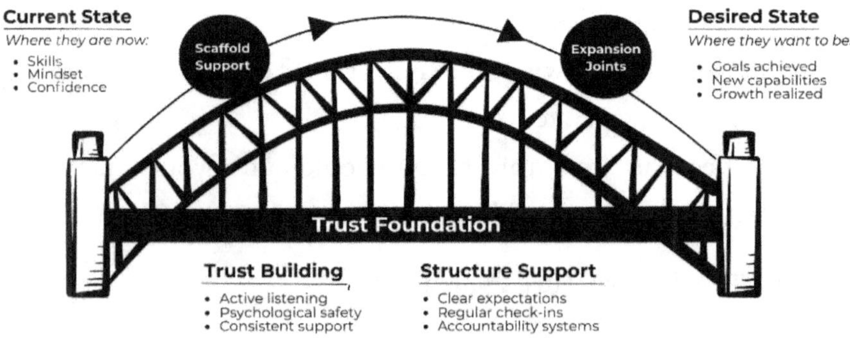

Figure 2.2 – Bridge Building Practice: Mapping the Path from Awareness to Action

Reflection Questions

- As you reflect on your own position in enabling others to grow, where do the boundaries seem clearest to you between AI assistance, therapy, and coaching?
- How do you currently balance efficiency and compassion in your leadership or coaching approach?
- What does "presence" mean to you in professional relationships, and how can technology contribute to or detract from it?
- Under what circumstances do you find yourself most wanting to provide quick answers instead of seeking further inquiry?

Moving Forward

The lines of coaching, therapy, and AI/technology will continue to move as technology and human needs evolve. The one constant is the need to know what each modality can provide and when one or the other is best indicated.

Coaching holds a special place in this landscape, future-oriented and yet rooted in current reality, planned and yet adaptive, data-driven and yet relationally dense. As AI assumes more routine functions and delivers increasingly advanced analysis, coaches are more valuable for what only humans can offer: the capacity to sit with complexity, to hold space for emergence, and to facilitate transformation through authentic connection.

The infrastructure metaphor also reminds us that coaching is not a luxury or add-on service. It is foundational support that enables individuals and organizations to weather change while preserving their structural integrity. Just as buildings require both firm foundations and pliable joints to survive earthquakes, individuals require both stable support and adaptive guidance to flourish in the midst of disruption.

The next chapter addresses how cultural responsiveness must be built into this infrastructure from the outset. We'll examine why coaching that does not account for identity, power, and systemic context can't possibly enable our diverse leaders to lead us through our ever more complex world.

Culturally Responsive Coaching in a Technological World

Jamal Richardson was in his sixth year as an executive coach when a pharmaceutical company brought him in to help with their diversity initiative. As one of the few Black coaches in their vendor network, and one of even fewer who had grown up in Detroit's east side before earning his psychology PhD from Northwestern, he had welcomed the chance to work with leaders who looked like the communities he came from. But three months into the project, he was becoming increasingly uncomfortable with something much deeper than individual client challenges.

The AI-powered coaching software the firm utilized wasn't just delivering misaligned insights. It was perpetuating the very systemic barriers his clients faced daily. Amara was a brilliant Indian–American scientist whose quiet strength had earned her a senior research role despite being passed over for promotions twice. When Jamal coached her, the AI marked Amara's communication style as "passive" and suggested assertiveness training. David was a Latino marketing director whose collaborative energy had transformed three underperforming teams, achieved while he navigated constant microaggressions about his "cultural fit". The AI advised him to "tone down emotional expressions" to appear more professional.

In a scheduled peer-reflection meeting with Robin, a fellow coach using the same platform, Jamal raised what felt like a professional crisis. "I'm not just battling the system in every session," he said, stirring his coffee with unusual intensity. "I'm watching technology reproduce the exact biases that made my clients' careers harder in the first place."

Robin leaned forward, her expression shifting. "I've noticed some of those patterns myself, but honestly, I didn't know if I was seeing it clearly. What do you think is really happening here?"

"The AI is learning from decades of leadership data that excluded people like us," Jamal explained. "When Amara sets boundaries, which she's had to learn to do after years of being overlooked, the system reads it as weakness because it's comparing her to leadership models built by and for people who never had to prove their worth twice. When David shows passion, it flags unprofessionalism because the algorithm was trained on cultures where only certain people were allowed to express authentic emotion without being labeled as 'too much.'"

Robin set down her cup. "So, we're not just dealing with individual coaching challenges. We're dealing with technology that's systematically misreading cultural strengths as professional deficits."

"Exactly. And here's the thing that keeps me up at night," Jamal continued. "These aren't just bad recommendations. They're asking my clients to diminish the very qualities that make them effective leaders in diverse environments, the same qualities their organizations claim to value."

"What do we do?" Robin asked. "The company loves the data insights, and honestly, some of the analytics are genuinely helpful."

Jamal paused, then smiled for the first time in their conversation. "We flip the script. Instead of letting the AI drive our understanding, we use it as raw material for deeper questions."

Over the following months, Jamal developed what he called his cultural translation framework: a three-step process that transformed how he approached AI-generated insights:

1. Validate the AI-generated theme: Rather than accepting or rejecting the observation, he would explore it with genuine curiosity. "The system is flagging something about your communication style. Let's examine what it might be picking up on."

2. Contextualize the behavior within the client's lived identity: He would explore the cultural, historical, and systemic factors shaping both the behavior and how it was being perceived. "Given your experience as one of the few Latino executives in this company, how might your leadership style be landing differently than intended?"

3. Co-create strengths-based language to navigate systemic misunderstanding: Together, they would develop strategies that honored the client's authentic self while building skills to navigate biased organizational cultures.

The transformation in his sessions was remarkable. When the AI flagged Amara's reflective approach as "passive," Jamal helped her reframe her contemplative leadership style as strategic depth that prevented costly rushed decisions. "Your thoughtfulness isn't a weakness to overcome," he told her during one session. "It's a competitive advantage this organization desperately needs. The question is: how do we help them recognize it?"

With David, when the AI suggested toning down his expressiveness, they worked together to understand how his authentic passion could be strategically deployed. "Your energy transforms teams," Jamal reflected. "But you're navigating a system that's been trained to misread cultural expressiveness as unprofessionalism. How do we honor your authentic leadership while building your skills to code-switch when strategic?"

Both leaders didn't just become more effective; they became more confident. Amara began speaking up earlier in meetings, framing her reflective insights as strategic analysis. David learned to calibrate his expressiveness across different organizational contexts while refusing to diminish his collaborative warmth.

Perhaps most importantly, they both developed what Jamal called "systemic literacy"—the ability to recognize when organizational resistance to their leadership wasn't about their capabilities, but about cultural biases embedded in systems and structures.

The ripple effects extended beyond individual transformation. As Amara and David became more effective advocates for their own leadership styles, they began creating space for other leaders from underrepresented communities to show up authentically, gradually shifting the cultural norms of their teams and divisions.

Six months later, when the pharmaceutical company asked Jamal to train other coaches in his approach, he realized his cultural translation framework had become something larger: a methodology for using technology to surface bias rather than perpetuate it, and for coaching leaders not just to succeed within existing systems, but to gradually transform them.

* * *

Just like Jamal, you might be feeling uncomfortable with how technology seems to push everyone toward the same narrow definition of success, overlooking the rich diversity of leadership styles and cultural strengths that different people bring. Luckily, this chapter will equip you with the tools to recognize and interrupt cultural bias in AI systems, honor the full complexity of your clients' identities, and create coaching practices that celebrate authentic leadership rather than forcing conformity to outdated standards.

The Cultural Dimension of Transformative Coaching

In a society obsessed with optimization, coaching can easily become another performance hack. A tool to help employees do more with less. A checkbox on a leadership development agenda.

But the coaching that transforms people and systems requires more than clever goals and accountability frameworks. It requires an understanding of identity, power, culture, and context.

That's where culturally responsive coaching becomes essential.

And in a world increasingly shaped by artificial intelligence, it is not just essential; it is non-negotiable.

Consider cultural responsiveness to be the engineering test that makes infrastructure safe to serve diverse communities. City planners don't make assumptions about how people travel, their mobility requirements, or access challenges when they plan transportation systems. They use demographic analysis, community hearings, and equity impact analysis to make sure the infrastructure works for all.

Organizational infrastructure requires the same level of cultural engineering. The systems that support human development—leadership development programs, feedback mechanisms, coaching discussions— must be designed with different starting points, different challenges, and different definitions of success in mind.

Absent such cultural engineering, even benevolent infrastructure can be exclusionary. A bridge that is only wide enough for some types of vehicles welcomes some travelers and bars others. Likewise, coaching styles that only value specific leadership approaches or communication styles uplift some individuals and limit others.

Cultural responsiveness is the diagnostic and design principle that makes human infrastructure function for all the populations it's designed to serve.

What Is Culturally Responsive Coaching?

Culturally responsive coaching is not a niche approach; it is a fundamental approach to coaching. It's not just for DEI roles. It's not about perfect language or performative political correctness. It's about coaching people with full awareness of who they are, where they come from, and what systems they're navigating

Let's break each of these down further.

Listening for Identity

Listening for identity involves attending to the ways in which cultural background informs a client's worldview, communication style, and leadership style. For example, imagine a first-generation college graduate who heads a technical team, who describes feeling out of place in executive meetings, and a culturally responsive coach inquires about what that experience means in his particular context. Instead of rushing into confidence-building exercises, they look at how class dynamics, education, and family expectations shape the client's experience of leadership authority.

Think of an Asian woman in finance who is told she's too quiet during leadership meetings. A culturally responsive coach might explore how cultural norms around respect, hierarchy, or speaking order are being misinterpreted as disengagement, and how she might navigate these perceptions while staying true to her leadership style.

Honoring Lived Experience

Traditional coaching may group all clients together as if they face the same workplace realities. Culturally responsive coaching recognizes that being Black and navigating organizational life, or being a working parent, or having a visible disability, or being a non-native English speaker brings unique challenges that must be acknowledged and worked with.

For instance, consider a Japanese manager who describes his preference for building consensus before making decisions. A culturally responsive coach would not frame this as indecisiveness to be fixed. Instead, they would explore how his value of collective harmony, rooted in cultural norms, can be positioned as a leadership asset. Together, they would work on ways to express this approach effectively in fast-paced American business environments where decisiveness is often prioritized.

Rather than seeing cultural differences as a gap to overcome, the coach sees it as an opportunity to co-create new strategies that respect both the client's identity and the system's demands.

Questioning Systems, Not Just Individuals

Rather than asking, "How can you change to be a better fit?" culturally responsive coaching asks, "What is it about this system that may be generating barriers for individuals like you?" This system's perspective uncovers how organizational culture, policies, and informal networks disadvantage some groups and privilege others.

Consider a Muslim woman who wears a hijab and is finding it difficult to build professional relationships in a workplace where networking happens primarily at after-hours events that involve alcohol. A culturally responsive coach would not frame this as a networking challenge she needs to overcome. Instead, the coach would explore how she can build meaningful professional connections in ways that honor her values and how she might advocate for more inclusive networking practices within the organization.

It's not about helping her adapt to exclusionary norms. It's about helping her lead change from within, while staying true to her identity.

Supporting the Client's Entire Humanity,
Not Only Their Performance

This principle affirms that work performance cannot be separated from personal identity, family responsibilities, immigration experiences, economic pressures, or community roles. When coaching artificially divides the professional from the personal, it often asks individuals to fragment themselves in ways that ultimately undermine long-term success and well-being.

Consider a Latino director who is financially supporting extended family members. A culturally responsive coach doesn't frame these responsibilities as distractions from leadership growth. Instead, the coach explores how these obligations inform his career choices, values, and sources of stress, then works with him to integrate those realities into a sustainable leadership approach.

Coaching that ignores cultural context or lived complexity risks reinforcing the very systems it claims to disrupt.

The Risk of Culturally Blind AI

As we introduced in the previous chapter, AI systems, by default, are trained on historical data. Historical data is also full of bias. That means AI tools can easily reproduce:

- Gendered assumptions about leadership
- Racialized language about performance or potential
- Eurocentric models of communication, influence, or success

Without culturally responsive coaching frameworks, AI-augmented coaching risks amplifying harm under the guise of efficiency.

Imagine an AI journaling assistant that misinterprets a client's boundary-setting as lack of collaboration. Or a feedback tool that flags assertiveness in a woman of color as aggression. These aren't hypotheticals. They're historical patterns, now being coded into data.

Research Reveals the Difference Between Data and Understanding

The research substantiates these concerns with tangible accuracy. MIT studies have determined that facial recognition technology has much greater error rates for darker-skinned women, an astonishing 34.7% error rate. The error rate is 0.8% for lighter-skinned men (Hardesty, 2018).

Stanford research illustrated how AI résumé screening software routinely penalizes job applications from women for tech jobs based on what it has learned from historical hiring patterns in which male candidates were overwhelmingly selected.

Amazon's prototype hiring algorithm had to be abandoned after it was found to discriminate against women, having taught itself that male-dominated hiring trends constituted the "ideal" candidate profile (Goodman, 2018). The tool systematically disadvantaged candidates from women's colleges and downgraded résumés containing terms like "women's," while privileging language patterns typically used by men, such as action verbs like "executed" and "captured" (Goodman, 2018).

Those biases are not system bugs. Unfortunately, they are features the AI discovered from decades of biased human judgments.

This pattern of biased algorithmic decision-making extends beyond hiring and performance reviews into other domains where media representation shapes public perception. Research has demonstrated that women politicians receive significantly less media visibility than their male counterparts in certain electoral systems, with studies showing women politicians receive approximately 17 percentage points less media attention in proportional representation systems (Van der Pas et al., 2020).

When coaching platforms include the same AI tools for theme analysis, sentiment monitoring, or development prescriptions, they potentially amplify those identical patterns in the name of objective insight.

This challenge extends beyond individual hiring decisions to systemic organizational practices. Research demonstrates that while AI can potentially mitigate human bias in employment decisions, it requires careful implementation to avoid reproducing historical discrimination patterns, as organizations using responsible AI practices have shown measurable increases in diversity hiring rates (Houser, 2019).

That's why the 5-Phase model always centers human interpretation, psychological safety, and identity-based context as non-negotiable components of coaching.

Cultural Fluency as Leadership Capacity

The best coaches are not just question-askers. They are pattern recognizers, context holders, and space makers. And in a time when organizations are navigating generational shifts, racial reckoning, and global hybrid workforces, culturally fluent coaching is no longer a competitive advantage; it's a leadership imperative.

This fluency will be even more critical when AI enters the coaching room. Coaches will need to:

- Challenge outputs that lack nuance
- Translate tools into culturally grounded practices
- Elevate human insight over machine-generated insight

Growth cannot be separated from context.
Behavior cannot be separated from identity.
Development cannot be separated from equity.

These truths must remain at the center of any coaching model that hopes to thrive in the age of AI.

Reclaiming Coaching's Purpose

The purpose of coaching is not just to drive better performance. It is to create space for reflection, reimagining, and radical growth for individuals and institutions.

Culturally responsive coaching reminds us that:

- Coaching is not about standardization. It's about transformation.
- Listening is not passive. It's a political act.
- Context is not a barrier. It's the birthplace of meaning.

Illustrative Example

Take the example of Lin, a high-performing engineer from Taiwan who was promoted to lead a global software development team. Shortly after her promotion, her manager noticed a drop in productivity metrics and sought coaching support. Here is how two contrasting approaches played out:

Scenario 1: AI-Only Approach

The AI coaching platform analyzed Lin's meeting participation, communication patterns, and team feedback. It flagged that she spoke less than previous team leaders, gave indirect feedback, and took longer to make decisions. Based on this, it recommended assertiveness training, decision-making workshops, and executive presence coaching. The development plan emphasized speaking more, being direct, and accelerating decision-making

Scenario 2: AI + Culturally Responsive Coaching

While the same AI-generated data was reviewed, Lin's coach began with a different entry point:

"Tell me about your leadership philosophy, and how your background and values shape your style."

That conversation revealed that Lin's reflective decision-making honored a cultural value of considering multiple perspectives before acting. Her indirect feedback style was grounded in a deep respect for relational harmony and emotional safety.

Rather than encouraging Lin to override her instincts, the coach helped her translate them. Together, they reframed her approach as "comprehensive input gathering" rather than indecision, and practiced strategies for offering constructive feedback that honored both her team relationships and her organizational expectations.

This highlights a common pattern. In the first scenario, Lin felt pressure to abandon her identity in favor of a dominant leadership mold. Her confidence declined, and so did her effectiveness.

In the second, Lin became more self-assured and agile. Her leadership felt authentic. Her team thrived under her culturally grounded approach, reporting stronger collaboration and deeper psychological safety than they had experienced under previous leaders who had followed Western executive norms.

The same data. Two vastly different outcomes.

The difference wasn't in the analysis. It was in the interpretation and coaching mindset behind it.

Chapter 3 Practice Lab

Activity 1: Cultural Context Mapping

- Think of an individual whom you are coaching or mentoring currently (or yourself, if you are examining your own development).
- Create a basic map with three circles:
    - Identity Circle: Enumerate important aspects of their cultural identity (race, gender, generation, socioeconomic status, etc.)
    - System Circle: Note the organizational or cultural systems they navigate daily
    - Intersection Circle: Identify points where their identity aligns with or pushes against system expectations, norms, or pressures
- Consider how these intersections could influence their leadership style, communication style, or work experience.

Cultural Context Mapping

Explore the relationship between identity and systems

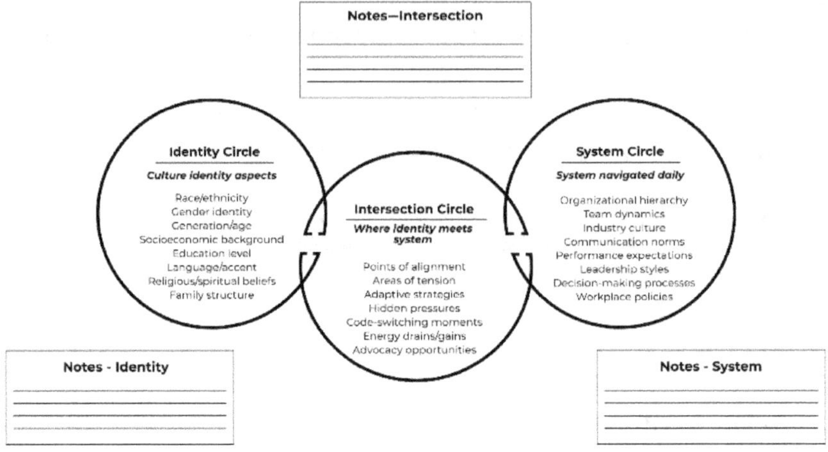

Figure 3.1 – Cultural Context Mapping

Activity 2: Practicing Bias Interrupts

- Reflect on a recent moment when you interpreted someone's behavior. What assumptions did you make, and what might you have missed?

- Write down:
    - What you observed (facts only)
    - What you believed was the reason why they acted that way
    - What cultural or identity issues you did not consider initially
    - How your interpretation would be different with more cultural context

- Practice saying: "What cultural context could account differently for this interpretation?" before jumping to conclusions.

Activity 3: Infrastructure Equity Audit

- Assess a development program, feedback mechanism, or coaching method in your firm:
    - Whose leadership styles are rewarded or recognized?
    - What communication norms are deemed effective?
    - What cultural values are implied or prioritized?
    - Who might be left out or disadvantaged by this structure?
    - What changes could make it more inclusive or responsive?

Reflection Questions

- In what ways has your own cultural heritage influenced your presumptions regarding effective leadership or communication?
- When using AI tools or data analysis, what are some questions you ask to ensure that cultural context is taken into account?
- What aspects of your identity do you unapologetically bring to your leadership or coaching practice, and what do you minimize?
- What do you currently treat as "universal" in leadership, and how might that assumption be culturally shaped?
- In what ways can the systems within which you work privilege certain cultural approaches over others?
- In what ways would your coaching practice change if you consistently placed cultural context at the forefront and not as an afterthought?

Moving Forward

Cultural responsiveness transforms coaching from a standardized intervention into a dynamic partnership that honors the full complexity of human experience. As AI tools become more sophisticated and more widely adopted, the need for this human discernment becomes increasingly critical.

The metaphor of infrastructure helps us remember that systems that are not designed with culture in mind necessarily exclude or marginalize some communities while benefiting others. Just as city planners now acknowledge that "neutral" design tends to reproduce inequality, coaches need to learn that "colorblind" or "culture-neutral" practice tends to entrench rather than remedy existing bias.

This neither renders coaching less effective nor more complex. On the contrary, it renders it more accurate and more powerful because it works with the real conditions under which people develop and lead. Honoring cultural context doesn't add complexity; it demands that we coach in reality, not abstraction.

The integration of AI into coaching magnifies both opportunity and risk. It can reveal macro-level cultural trends that a single coach might miss. But it can also entrench stereotypes, misread identity, and flatten nuance when its training data lacks diversity.

That's why coaches must not rely on AI passively. We must engage critically, questioning its assumptions, contextualizing its insights, and placing human discernment above algorithmic suggestion.

The solution is not to avoid AI tools, then, but to engage with them through a culturally responsive lens that questions assumptions, critiques results, and prioritizes human interpretation over algorithmic recommendations.

The groundwork is laid. We've defined what coaching is and is not, why cultural responsiveness is not optional, and how these frameworks provide the foundation necessary for integrating AI ethically. But awareness of systems and identity is only part of the equation. To sustain this work in practice, leaders also need the inner capacity to recognize their own emotions, regulate their responses, and connect authentically with others under pressure.

As we transition to Part II: Human Skills for the AI Era, we make the shift from conceptual knowledge to capability building. The following section examines the uniquely human skills that grow more valuable, not less, as routine tasks are managed by artificial intelligence.

We begin with emotional intelligence, the foundation that facilitates culturally responsive coaching and the skill that will likely be most vital in our tech-enabled future. We examine why EI becomes even more critical in AI-augmented environments and how coaches can develop this capacity in concert with the technological fluency required to coach others through digital transformation will be addressed in Part II.

PART II
HUMAN SKILLS FOR THE AI ERA

The paradox of technological progress is revealing itself: the more machines are able to do routine cognitive tasks, the more valuable uniquely human abilities are, not less.

We're seeing this transition happen across fields. Radiologists are transitioning from pattern recognition to complicated case consultation as AI takes over initial screenings. Financial planners are transitioning from portfolio management to emotional advising as algorithms maximize investment approaches. Educators are transforming from information dissemination to critical thinking facilitation as AI delivers customized content.

The same shift is occurring in leadership development and coaching. As AI solutions take over data analysis, schedule optimization, and even the generation of basic feedback, the human aspects that appeared "soft" are emerging as the most difficult competitive differentiators to duplicate.

Part II is concerned with cultivating these indispensable human abilities, not in opposition to, but in anticipation of, technological evolution, as intentional preparation for leadership in an AI-enhanced world.

- *Chapter 4: Emotional Intelligence Is the New Tech Literacy* positions EI as the baseline for all else. We discuss why emotional awareness, regulation, and empathy become increasingly important when algorithms inform decision-making. You'll learn how emotionally intelligent coaches can navigate clients through the psychological nuances of human–AI collaboration and hold authentic relationships in ever more digital spaces.

- *Chapter 5: The ICI Framework: 3 Models for Ethical AI Integration* provides practical frameworks for blending human insight with technological promise. We discuss the augmented coaching integration (ACI) model, the AI-enhanced coaching (AIEC) framework, and the comprehensive ICI 5-Phase Model. These are not theoretical models. They are field-tested approaches developed through real-world application with diverse client populations.

- *Chapter 6: When AI Enters the Coaching Room* deals with the immediate practical issues coaches need to confront today. How do you preserve presence when algorithms are delivering insights? What do you do when clients come with AI-generated self-assessments? How do you weigh efficiency against empathy when technology promises instant solutions? In this chapter, you'll find concrete strategies for working with these new realities.

Together, these three chapters address a fundamental question: What are the human skills that leaders and coaches must acquire in order to remain relevant and valuable as AI continues to develop?

The solution is not to get more technical. It's about getting more profoundly human.

Think of this chapter as specialized training for the unique challenges of human–AI teamwork. Just as astronauts need specialized abilities for zero-gravity environments, leaders who deal with AI integration need specialized abilities for technological environments that both enhance human potential and human complexity.

The competencies in Part II are not supplements to classical leadership skills; they're the technologically adapted versions of age-old human abilities. Emotional intelligence is what serves as the interface between human values and algorithmic suggestions. Ethical reasoning is what acts as the guardrail so that efficiency does not trump empathy. Cultural responsiveness is what functions as the quality control system so that AI bias does not perpetuate workplace injustices.

Every chapter contains diagnostic instruments to enable you to evaluate your present ability in these domains, development exercises that enhance these skills through practice, and integration strategies that assist you in putting these abilities into practice in your individual work situation.

Whether you are a professional coach transforming your practice for AI-enhanced clients, a leader cultivating these capabilities for your own development, or an organizational developer constructing capability throughout teams, Part II offers the human skill base required for technological integration that supports people and strengthens human leadership.

The future is for those who can think like a human and collaborate with machines. Part II assists you in cultivating the human half of that calculation with accuracy, intent, and cultural insight.

Your tech tools will keep changing. Your human skills will dictate how well you're able to lead others through that change.

Emotional Intelligence Is the New Tech Literacy

Leila Haddad, a Lebanese product director at a global healthcare company, had always been proud of her stamina. She built her reputation on being reliable, the one who stayed late, answered emails at midnight, and never missed a deadline. When her company adopted an AI-driven "leadership sentiment tracker" to analyze communication patterns, Leila barely paid attention.

But one Monday morning, the AI dashboard caught her off guard. Next to her name, a bright orange alert read: "At risk for burnout."

She frowned. Burnout? That didn't feel true. She was tired, yes, but she had always been tired. That was leadership.

Still, the tool listed examples from her emails:

"I'll try to get this done before the meeting."

"Sorry for the delay."

"I know it's late, but I wanted to get this to you tonight."

Seeing the words reflected unsettled her more than she expected. She closed the dashboard quickly, muttering, "That's just how I write."

When she brought it up with her coach, she laughed it off. "The AI thinks I'm burned out. I'm not. I just work hard."

Her coach paused, letting the words settle before asking, "What do you notice about the language it flagged?"

Leila hesitated. "I guess I apologize a lot. And … I soften things. I don't want to sound bossy."

"Where do you think that comes from?"

The question landed. For the first time, Leila admitted what she had never put into words: after years of being one of the only women of color in senior meetings, she had internalized the need to over-explain and over-extend, to prove she belonged. Her late-night emails weren't just about catching up. They were a survival strategy.

"I didn't realize how much of my exhaustion was showing through," she said slowly. "The AI gave me the signals. But you helped me see the story behind them."

Together, they reframed her habits. Instead of "I'll try to get this done," she began writing "I will deliver this by Friday." Instead of apologizing for normal delays, she set clearer expectations. And instead of sending midnight emails, she drafted them and scheduled delivery for the morning.

Within weeks, her team noticed the difference. Meetings felt calmer. Her updates were clearer. And for the first time in years, Leila herself felt less like she was running on fumes.

The AI had spotted the pattern. But it was coaching, and Leila's new self-awareness, that transformed it into growth.

Leila's story illustrates a simple truth: the patterns that matter most in leadership are not just technical; they're emotional. And in today's AI-augmented world, the ability to recognize, interpret, and respond to those emotional signals is not optional. It is foundational.

This capacity is known as emotional intelligence (EI). Sometimes it's referred to as EQ, an emotional quotient meant to mirror the idea of intelligence quotient, or IQ. But EI is not about how much you know; it's about how well you understand and manage emotions in yourself and others. In this book, we'll use the more accurate term EI.

Psychologist Daniel Goleman's pioneering work made EI a household term in leadership development. His model outlines four core domains: self-awareness, self-management, social awareness, and relationship management. These domains provide the framework we'll use to explore how emotionally intelligent coaching helps leaders thrive in a technology-driven environment.

When we talk about the skills needed to thrive in the age of AI, we usually hear a familiar list:

Coding. Data analysis. Prompt engineering. Digital fluency.

These technical skills matter. But they are not what ultimately defines effective leadership. As machines become better at thinking, calculating, and even simulating emotion, the most irreplaceable human skill is no longer technical. It's emotional.

Emotional intelligence is no longer a "soft skill."

It's the essential skill for leading, coaching, and creating in a world saturated with artificial intelligence.

What Is Emotional Intelligence?

Daniel Goleman's seminal work during the 1990s made emotional intelligence a key leadership skill. His research suggested that EI could account for a significant share of job performance, some studies estimating as high as 58%, and that a large majority of high performers also scored high in EI (Goleman, 2005). More recent studies have confirmed these results in various cultural contexts, demonstrating that emotionally intelligent leaders foster psychological safety, enhance team performance, and lead change more successfully (Ertiö et al., 2024).

Goleman specified four domains of emotional intelligence:

1. Self-awareness – Being aware of your feelings at the moment they arise and how they affect your thoughts and actions. In coaching, this means being aware of your personal triggers, biases, and emotional reactions in sessions.

2. Self-management – The capacity to manage disruptive impulses and emotions and remain focused and flexible. Coaches who exhibit self-management are able to remain present with clients even in difficult conversations.

3. Social awareness – Accurately perceiving other individuals' emotions and understanding group dynamics. It entails empathy, the ability to understand and share another person's emotions.

4. Relationship management – Utilizing emotional intelligence to enable interactions, build rapport, and achieve positive outcomes. In the case of coaches, this means creating the conditions for trust and transformation.

In coaching, these aspects are fundamental. They inform how we hold space, how we inquire, and how we reflect language and energy. Yet in an AI world, they are even more essential.

Why Emotional Intelligence Now?

In 2025, *Harvard Business Review* reported that one of the top three uses of generative AI was not business strategy, analytics, or scheduling, but emotional support.

This finding aligns with a broader trend. While organizations invest heavily in AI to analyze data and optimize efficiency, employees are increasingly using the same tools to manage their inner worlds. A 2024 McKinsey survey, cited in Mayer et al. (2025), found that 34% of employees turned to AI chatbots for work-related stress management, 28% for decision support, and 22% for conflict resolution.

In practice, people are using AI to:

- Process emotions: Putting feelings into words when no trusted listener is available
- Navigate conflict: Rehearsing conversations or testing different phrasings
- Reflect on decisions: Checking thinking patterns or weighing alternatives
- Cope with uncertainty: Seeking reassurance or perspective when the future feels unstable

The desire is genuine. The tools are efficient. Yet the need remains profoundly human. That is where emotionally intelligent coaches step in.

Consider the infrastructure metaphor that runs throughout this book. When a city grows quickly, its road systems, water supply, and electrical grid face increased demand. Unless they are reinforced, they buckle under pressure. Similarly, as AI takes on more routine cognitive tasks, the emotional infrastructure of organizations is placed under strain.

Leaders and employees alike need more help metabolizing change, negotiating complex relationships, and making sense of evolving roles. Emotional intelligence functions as the load-bearing beam of this infrastructure. It distributes emotional stress across the system, prevents overload at fragile connection points, and provides structural integrity in times of rapid change and in an AI-driven era, it is nothing less than essential.

EI as a Coaching Superpower in the Age of AI

Emotionally intelligent coaches bring capabilities that no algorithm can replicate. They demonstrate:

- Listening beyond the data. AI tools can flag sentiment in text, but they cannot perceive the subtle pause before a client says, "I'm fine," or the shift in energy when a certain colleague is mentioned. Coaches who listen with presence translate faint signals into meaningful insight. This reflects the *awareness* pillar of coaching.

- Building human bridges. In distributed and AI-mediated workplaces, genuine connection is rare. Coaches who can hold space, build rapport, and create relational safety counterbalance digital overwhelm. This ensures clients retain *choice* in how they relate to themselves and others.

- Modeling emotional regulation. In systems that reward speed and output, the ability to slow down, reflect, and respond thoughtfully becomes a competitive edge. Coaches show that emotional regulation is not about suppressing feelings, but about judiciously applying emotional information. This demonstrates *integration*, aligning emotional insight with wise action.

- Navigating cross-cultural dynamics. AI tools often misinterpret culturally diverse emotional expressions. A coach who understands that directness may be valued in one culture and harmony in another can help leaders interpret these differences with empathy and skill.

For example, consider Dr. Aisha Patel, an executive coach supporting a global technology team. The team's AI analytics flagged certain members as low engagement based on their limited verbal participation in meetings. When Dr. Patel met with them individually, she discovered the opposite: these members were highly engaged through active listening and nonverbal feedback, behaviors common in high-context cultures but invisible to the algorithm. Instead of coaching them to speak more, she coached the team leader to recognize and leverage multiple participation styles.

As AI enters the coaching profession, through journaling assistants, diagnostic tools, or synthesized feedback, the coach's superpower is to re-humanize what machines flatten. Leading with sensitivity to how emotion is expressed across diverse identities and systems is not optional. It is the heart of ethical, culturally responsive coaching in the age of AI.

Emotional Intelligence Is Cultural Intelligence

Emotional intelligence must always be culturally grounded. What is considered assertive in one culture may be perceived as disrespectful in another. Emotional expression is never universal.

Coaches must learn to navigate:

- Power dynamics in multicultural teams that are characterized by the expression of hierarchy and voice in different ways
- Generational interpretations of feedback or vulnerability, where one group may see openness as a strength while another sees it as a weakness
- Identity-based trauma responses that AI tools cannot reliably detect or hold space for

This is where training matters. This is where coach education must evolve. And this is where ICI's model, integrating emotional intelligence into every phase of AI innovation, stands out. Through *awareness*, *choice*, and *integration*, coaches can contextualize AI outputs within culture, not apart from it.

The Emotional Landscape of AI

It is tempting to think of AI as cold, technical, or neutral. Yet it is entering a world overflowing with human complexity. And that complexity will not be solved by more intelligent algorithms.

It will be supported by emotionally intelligent leaders, coaches, and educators who can hold space for:

- Fear of being replaced
- Fatigue from constant change
- Frustration with dehumanizing systems
- Hope for a more just, inclusive future

In a world where machines are being trained to think, coaches must be the ones who feel. Emotional intelligence is not just another skill. It is the soul of coaching and the foundation on which the next chapter of AI integration must be built.

Illustrative Case:
Phase 1 – Building Trust Before the First Session

Title: *Beyond the Welcome Packet: Using AI to Support Readiness and Rapport*

Challenge:

A large healthcare organization was onboarding a cohort of 60 mid-level managers into their first-ever coaching program. Participants came from various cultural and professional backgrounds, with limited exposure to coaching. Early feedback revealed high levels of uncertainty about what coaching entailed and anxiety about what to expect.

Context:

Imagine this organization partnering with ICI to ensure that participants felt psychologically safe and prepared before their first session. In today's model, intake relies primarily on forms and coach review, which can leave coaches with little context about participants' emotional state or readiness. In a future-facing scenario, lightweight AI-powered support tools could complement these processes.

Coaching Engagement (Scenario):

In this example, an AI-powered intake assistant might answer common questions about coaching, privacy, and goal setting. It could also offer short reflective prompts based on participants' self-assessment scores, generating a one-page readiness brief (not diagnostic, but narrative-based) for the coach. This would allow coaches to tailor their first sessions with greater sensitivity.

Transformation (Hypothetical):

Participants reported feeling seen even before their first session. One participant said, "I thought it was just going to be paperwork, but it felt like someone already understood what I needed." Coaches noted faster rapport-building and greater session depth from the very beginning.

Architectural Framework:

As with any accomplished building project, this venture required careful infrastructure planning:

- Clear foundations – The foundation rests on cultural understanding and trust. AI could be programmed with culturally responsive language and adapt to different levels of comfort with technology.
- Proper scaffolding – The AI tools served as scaffolding, enhancing the preparation process without replacing human connection. The chatbot could provide structure and content while coaches remained the primary relationship builders.

- Structural integrity – Ethical paradigms regulate all collection and use of data. Participants retain full agency over their information, and the AI assistant is built to augment and not substitute for human judgment.
- Successful completion – The result would be stronger first-session relationships, quicker trust establishment, and more productive first sessions, showing how AI can augment and not detract from the human aspects of coaching.

Link to ICI Phase 1:

This example illustrates how Phase 1 of ICI's 5-Phase Model could be applied. AI-powered support tools can reinforce inclusion, readiness, and trust without replacing the coach–client relationship.

Illustrative Example

Let us see how the same healthcare organization scenario might unfold under different approaches:

Scenario 1: AI-Only Approach

The company has a holistic AI onboarding platform that evaluates participant readiness, assigns goals to coaches through algorithmic analysis, and delivers automated preparation modules. Participants undergo digital assessments and receive AI-generated materials for standardized welcome packets.

Results: While efficient, participants report feeling processed rather than welcomed. Many express concerns about privacy and authenticity. Several participants withdraw from the program before their first session, citing discomfort with the impersonal approach.

In this scenario, the same AI tools are used, yet human coaches screen all AI-driven insights before they are shared with participants. Participants are personally contacted by a coach following digital intake, recognizing their individual histories and discussing personal concerns. The AI delivers data, but coaches deliver meaning and connection.

Results: Clients are more likely to feel both effectively prepared and personally attended to. Trust is built prior to the initial formal session, resulting in more profound and fruitful coaching relationships. The marriage of technological efficiency and human compassion yields an ideal onboarding process.

The distinction is not in the technology employed, but in the way human emotional intelligence directs its use.

Chapter 4 Practice Lab

Activity 1: EI Infrastructure Appraisal

Graph your current emotional intelligence across the four domains: self-awareness, self-management, social awareness, and relationship management.

On a piece of paper, draw four quadrants with those four domains as titles. In each quadrant, note:

- Your current strengths in this area
- Situations where you struggle
- Where AI tools (such as sentiment trackers or journaling apps) might highlight useful patterns
- Where AI tools might misinterpret your behaviors or context
- One specific skill you want to strengthen to reinforce your EI "infrastructure."

Activity 2: Cultural EI Audit

Reflect on a recent leadership interaction or coaching conversation. Write down:

- What emotional cues you observed (verbal and nonverbal)
- What cultural factors might have influenced the person's emotional expression
- What assumptions you made regarding their emotional state
- How your own cultural background might have impacted your interpretation
- What you noticed that AI might miss, and what AI might miss that *you also missed at first.*

Activity 3: AI–Human EI Integration

Select an AI tool you are using or planning to use (email analytics, mood tracking apps, transcription or communication assistants, etc.):

Evaluate:

- What emotional intelligence information does this tool reveal?
- What important human context is it missing?
- How could you use its information as a springboard for deeper emotional discovery with a client?
- What limits or ethical guardrails would you need to establish to ensure the coach–client relationship remains primary?

Reflection Questions

How has your own emotional intelligence been tested or reinforced by technology in your workplace?

How do you distinguish between genuine emotional connection and AI-simulated sympathy when offering support to others?

What cultural factors influence how you express and interpret emotions in professional settings? How might AI tools miss these nuances?

As you reflect on the "human infrastructure" of your organization, where is emotional intelligence most vital, and why?

In what ways has the pace of technological change affected your own emotional equilibrium? What practices help you remain grounded?

What would shift in your leadership or coaching if you treated emotional intelligence not as an add-on skill, but as core infrastructure for human thriving?

Moving Forward

Emotional intelligence provides the groundwork for every other skill and framework in this book. It is the diagnostic tool and the interpretive lens through which AI integration can be made ethical and effective. Without EI, data becomes detached, decisions become mechanical, and leaders risk losing the very human connection that makes coaching transformative.

What comes next is how that emotional groundwork supports the structural design of coaching in the AI era. The Institute for Coaching Innovation has developed three companion frameworks to guide this work: the augmented coaching integration (ACI) model for one-to-one engagements, the AI-enhanced coaching (AIEC) framework for organizational implementation, and the ICI 5-phase model for scaling adoption responsibly. Each offers a different vantage point, but all are anchored in the same principle: technology should augment, not replace, the human relationship at the center of coaching.

Think of EI as the foundation of a building. Strong walls and elegant architecture are impossible without a base that can hold the weight. The

ACI model, the AIEC framework, and the ICI 5-phase model are the blueprints and scaffolding that rise from that foundation. They create the ethical guardrails and design specifications necessary to ensure AI supports human thriving.

Technology will keep changing, but the human desire for emotional intelligence, cultural responsiveness, and genuine connection does not. Coaches who excel at EI in the AI era do not merely survive technological disruption; they lead others through it with wisdom, integrity, and hope.

PART III
COACHING IN PRACTICE

The bridge between theory and change is where practice occurs. You may comprehend emotional intelligence theoretically, grasp cultural responsiveness rationally, and acknowledge the possibility of AI tools logically. Yet, coaching only becomes impactful when these factors come together in actual dialogue with real individuals who have real issues.

Part III shifts from foundational knowledge to daily practice. Here, we discuss how coaches engage with the daily realities of AI-augmented practice while maintaining the human depth that makes coaching transformative.

The infrastructure-building metaphor is still prominent. In Parts I and II, we mapped the landscape and drafted the plans. Now we start the building itself: pouring concrete, putting in support systems, and stress-testing the structure under real-world conditions.

- *Chapter 5: The ICI Framework: 3 Models for Ethical AI Integration* lays out the architectural blueprints for responsible AI integration in coaching. You'll discover three detailed frameworks: the augmented coaching integration (ACI) model for one-to-one coaching relationships, the AI-enhanced coaching (AIEC) framework for organizational roll-out, and the complete 5-phase integration blueprint for integrating AI tools across coaching programs. These aren't theoretical models; they're field-tested blueprints developed through hundreds of coaching sessions and refined through diverse client engagements.

- *Chapter 6: When AI Enters the Coaching Room* deals with the immediate practical issues coaches need to handle today. What do you do when clients come with AI-generated self-assessments? How do you maintain presence when algorithms are providing real-time insights? When do you rely on machine analysis, and when do you rely on your intuition? This chapter offers tangible strategies for protecting the human aspects of coaching while drawing on technological capability.

- *Chapter 7: Scaling Without Sacrificing Humanity* addresses how coaching programs scale without compromising quality and cultural sensitivity. We examine the trade-off between efficiency and empathy, standardization and personalization. Through detailed case studies, you'll discover how organizations have successfully implemented AI-powered coaching at scale without sacrificing the relational depth that drives transformation.

- *Chapter 8: What Gets Measured in a Hybrid Coaching World* tackles the complex challenge of evaluation in AI-augmented coaching. How do you assess progress when both machine analysis and human wisdom inform the work? What metrics capture transformation without reducing people to data points? We explore measurement frameworks that respect both quantitative insight and qualitative growth.

Collectively, these four chapters respond to a core question: How do you integrate AI into coaching practice without losing what is fundamentally human about coaching?

The systems we are designing must be technologically sophisticated and culturally responsive, streamlined yet empathetic, scalable, and still deeply personal. This requires precision engineering, not of machines, but of relationships, processes, and practices that serve human flourishing.

Part III turns from principles to practice. Here you will find case studies, practical tools, and example scenarios that illustrate how coaches and organizations can navigate the ethical challenges that emerge when human wisdom collides with artificial intelligence.

The objective is not to be more technological. It's to be more skillfully human in a world where technology expands both our potential and our accountability. Part III shows how to construct that bridge one conversation, one relationship, one changed leader at a time.

The groundwork is firm. The design is complete. Now it's time to build.

The ICI Framework: 3 Models for Ethical AI Integration

Foundations alone cannot hold a structure. To build responsibly, we need blueprints and guardrails that show where technology belongs and where it does not. This chapter introduces three such frameworks, developed by ICI, to guide the ethical integration of AI into coaching. Before we explore them in detail, consider the following scenario, which highlights what's at stake when privacy and consent are not clearly designed.

Priya Malhotra, a South Asian HR director working for a multinational tech firm, was eager to join her company's new leadership coaching program. The program promised to pair human coaches with AI-powered insights, giving leaders the best of both worlds.

However, during onboarding, she noticed a line in the consent form: "All coaching transcripts will be analyzed by the AI system for leadership patterns."

Her stomach tightened. Coaching had always felt like a sanctuary, a rare space for vulnerability. Did this mean her private conversations would become company data?

In her first session, she brought it up nervously. "I don't know how honest I can be," she admitted. "If every word is stored and analyzed, what's left of trust?"

Her coach didn't rush in with reassurance. Instead, he set his pen down and asked simply, "What do you need in order to feel safe here?"

Priya thought for a long moment. "I need to know that my voice won't be used against me. That what I say here is for my growth, not for someone else's report."

Together, they reviewed the consent language and reframed how she would participate. Priya decided she would allow AI-generated summaries for her own reflection, but she declined company-level analytics. The coach reinforced that this choice was hers, not the organization's.

Over the next weeks, something shifted. With clear boundaries, Priya spoke more freely about her leadership challenges. She opened up about her doubts about a promotion, her struggle to balance assertiveness with cultural expectations and her fears of bias in the company's systems. Far from slowing her development, her decision to set limits deepened it.

Later, she told her coach, "Saying no to full data sharing was the first time I felt like this program respected me as a person, not a datapoint."

The AI offered tools. But it was consent, trust, and cultural safety that made real transformation possible.

* * *

The future of coaching lies not in choosing between human intuition and artificial intelligence, but in designing AI integration with intentionality, ethics, and cultural responsiveness. This chapter introduces three integrative frameworks developed by the Institute for Coaching Innovation to guide this critical work.

These models are grounded in ICI's research, coaching practice, and organizational case analysis across diverse cultural contexts. They are designed as practical blueprints for AI-augmented coaching infrastructure development frameworks that scale human potential while protecting what makes coaching essentially transformational.

As with any solid building project, ethical AI integration takes planning, the right materials, and competent execution. The three frameworks in this chapter offer the architectural direction, engineering requirements, and construction guidelines necessary to construct coaching systems that are technologically advanced yet profoundly human.

A Brief Description of the Three Models

- The augmented coaching integration (ACI) model provides the underlying structure for one-on-one coaching relationships. It sets the fundamental principles of awareness, choice, and integration that have to underlie any application of AI tools in individual coaching engagements. The model ensures that technology augments but does not substitute for the coach–client relationship.

- The AI-enhanced coaching (AIEC) framework gives the organizational implementation its structural framework. It delivers four pillars—awareness, integration, ethics, and collaboration—that facilitate the phased introduction of AI tools throughout coaching programs without compromising quality and cultural responsiveness.

- The 5-phase model lays out the construction sequence for expanding AI-powered coaching from pilot programs to company-wide adoption. It offers a blueprint for implementing technological enhancements incrementally while building the human infrastructure needed for ethical and sustainable integration.

Together, these three models address different aspects of the same fundamental question: How do you bring artificial intelligence into coaching in a way that enhances human wisdom rather than replacing it?

The Augmented Coaching Integration (ACI) Model

The augmented coaching integration (ACI) model is the foundation for any AI integration into coaching relationships. It rests on three pillars—awareness, choice, and integration—that ensure every technology-supported coaching engagement remains human-centered, transparent, and grounded in trust.

Think of these pillars as the bridge supports that carry the weight of the coaching relationship: strong enough to uphold trust, yet flexible enough to hold space for reflection, presence, and transformation.

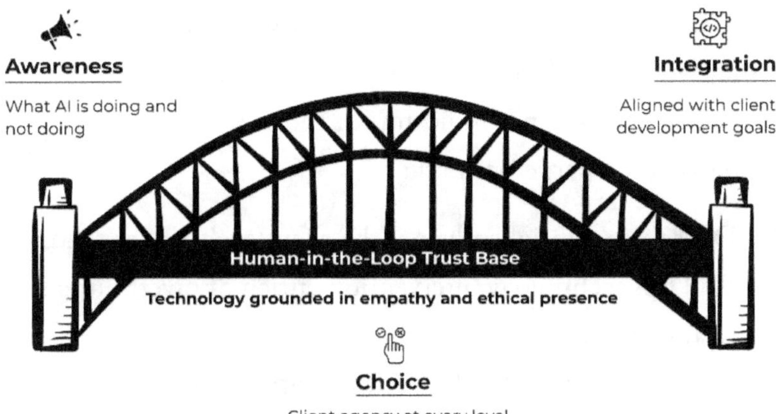

Figure 5.1 – The augmented coaching integration (ACI) model: The three pillars of awareness, choice, and integration rest on a human-in-the-loop trust base that grounds technology in empathy and ethical presence.

Pillar 1: Awareness – The coach and client are aware of what AI is doing and what it is not doing. This includes a shared understanding of:

- Which tools are being used and how they work.
- What information is being collected, analyzed, and retained
- Who has access to AI-derived summaries or insights

- How long data is retained and under what circumstances it might be shared
- What biases and limitations the AI tools might possess

Pillar 2: Choice – The client always has agency. They can engage AI in their development or decline it altogether. Choice must be meaningful, with equally effective non-AI options available. It includes:

- Initial choice: Decide whether to engage with AI tools at all
- Ongoing choice: Modify the level of AI engagement at any time
- Granular choice: Select certain AI capabilities while declining others
- Exit choice: Opt out of AI integration entirely without penalty

Pillar 3: Integration – AI outputs are integrated into coaching only when they align with the client's development agenda and not with the organization's performance indicators or the coach's convenience. This requires coaches to perpetually ask:

- Does this AI insight advance the client's self-understanding?
- Will this technology intervention enrich or divert our coaching relationship?
- Are we utilizing AI to look into complexity or oversimplify it?
- Who benefits most from this particular AI application?
- Throughout the process, the coach is always the human interpreter, guide, and presence source. Technology delivers data; coaches deliver meaning.

Illustrative Case: Reclaiming Authority in the Room

In one illustrative scenario, a senior engineering manager in a global tech firm found herself struggling to assert authority in cross-functional meetings. Despite being a technical expert, she routinely deferred to colleagues with stronger personalities and softened her opinions with phrases like, "I could be wrong, but..." or "Maybe another option is..."

Through coaching, she began to notice this pattern more clearly. Imagine pairing transcripts with lightweight AI-assisted analysis to surface recurring hedging language and frequent qualifiers. The data itself was neutral; it simply highlighted repetition. But when brought into the coaching space, those patterns became a mirror for deeper reflection.

Her coach transformed these insights into a series of journaling prompts and live practices around voice and presence: What do you lose when you soften your language? What would sound different if you owned your expertise outright? What story are you telling about who gets to take up space in the room?

As she experimented with these shifts, the leader reflected: "I didn't realize how much I gave away by apologizing for my perspective. Seeing the words on paper helped me hear myself differently. It gave me permission to be clearer."

Over time, she grew more declarative in meetings, used direct language in decision-making, and began coaching her own team members to speak with greater authority. AI revealed the pattern. Coaching helped her reauthor the story behind it.

This is what ethical augmentation **looks like in practice**: technology providing raw signals, with human coaches offering the interpretation, the meaning, and the path to transformation.

While the ACI model safeguards the intimacy and ethical integrity of one-to-one coaching relationships, organizations need a structure that applies those same principles at scale.

The next framework, the AI-enhanced coaching (AIEC) framework, extends this foundation across teams and systems, ensuring that ethics and cultural responsiveness grow along with technology.

The AI-Enhanced Coaching (AIEC) Framework

While the ACI model governs one-to-one coaching relationships, organizations need a structure that applies those same ethical principles at scale. The AI-enhanced coaching (AIEC) framework provides that structure. It outlines four pillars—awareness, integration, ethics, and collaboration—that guide ethical, inclusive, and sustainable AI integration across teams and systems. Think of these pillars as the engineering specifications that allow AI integration to scale without compromising structural integrity or human connection across diverse populations and settings.

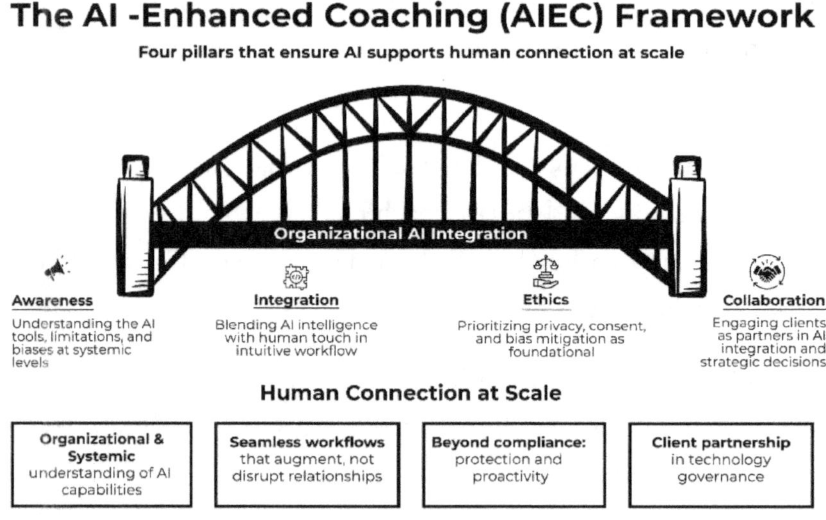

Figure 5.2 – The AI-enhanced coaching (AIEC) framework: The four pillars that ensure AI supports human connection at scale.

Pillar 1: Awareness – Organizations and coaches must be fully aware of their tools and their limitations at both the individual and systemic levels. These include:

- Understanding how AI algorithms generate recommendations and what data they prioritize.
- Identifying cultural, demographic, and contextual biases inherent in AI systems
- Staying current with emerging AI technology and ethical debates
- Training coaches to identify when AI outputs conflict with human wisdom or client needs

Pillar 2: Integration – Blend AI intelligence and human touch in intuitive and useful ways. Effective integration requires:

- Creating workflows that augment rather than disrupt the coaching relationship
- Ensuring smooth transitions from AI-generated insights to human interpretation
- Positioning technology as complementary, not competitive, to coach expertise
- Maintaining focus on relationship-building even when more data becomes available

Pillar 3: Ethics – Prioritize privacy, consent, and bias mitigation as foundational rather than optional elements. The ethics pillar encompasses:

- Applying strong data protection measures beyond what the law stipulates
- Establishing clear and adaptable consent processes clients can understand

- Conducting regular audits of AI tools for bias and taking corrective action when issues are found
- Creating accountability mechanisms for ethical violations or system failures

Pillar 4: Collaboration – Engage the clients to take an active role in AI integration as partners rather than passive consumers. Collaboration involves:

- Involving client feedback within decisions on tool selection and customization
- Offering clients a chance to influence the interpretation and implementation of AI findings
- Establishing regular review cycles where clients can assess the effectiveness of AI integration
- Allowing clients to propose adjustments or improvements to the organization's technology strategy

Together, these four pillars form the structural framework that enables AI to support rather than overshadow human connection in coaching.

The AIEC framework transforms AI insight into intercultural understanding, positioning coaches as translators between data and diversity. This framework doesn't replace the ICF core competencies; it enriches them by offering a future where technology and empathy must advance together.

AI may suggest, but coaches make meaning.

Illustrative Case: Bridging Cultural Gaps

A multinational technology firm faced challenges in enhancing collaboration between their Munich and Bangalore engineering teams.

Breakdowns in communication were common, project deadlines were slipping, and frustration was building on both sides.

In an illustrative scenario, coaches applied the AIEC framework to design a culturally sensitive intervention rather than impose a one-size-fits-all solution.

During the **awareness** phase, coaches identified that AI communication analysis tools had been trained primarily on Western business communication styles. The system persistently flagged the Indian team's context-rich communication as inefficient, while rating the German team's direct style as optimal.

Under **integration**, coaches worked with team leaders to examine how these styles actually influenced project outcomes. They found that the Indian team's elaborate explanations often prevented costly technical errors, while the German team's straightforwardness kept schedules on track.

The **ethics** pillar guided coaches to resist algorithmic recommendations that pushed toward standardization. Instead, they treated the AI findings as starting points for cross-cultural dialogue and reflection.

Through **collaboration**, both groups co-created communication protocols that balanced efficiency and relationship-building. The Indian team began including executive summaries alongside detailed explanations, and the German team allowed time for rapport-building in project schedules.

The AI surfaced useful information about communication patterns. But it was the coaches who provided the cultural intelligence and systemic insight to transform that information into improved collaboration.

Once both relational and organizational integrity are in place, the final step is to operationalize them.

The ICI 5-phase model provides the construction schedule for doing so, a roadmap that guides organizations from pilot programs to enterprise-wide, AI-supported coaching ecosystems.

ICI 5-Phase Model

While the AIEC framework describes the governing principles for responsible adoption, the ICI 5-phase model translates those principles into action, showing how human oversight and technological capability can be built layer by layer without compromising inclusion or trust.

The ICI 5-phase model is designed to provide a construction schedule for organizations looking to scale AI-powered coaching in a responsible way. As with any significant infrastructure project, this rollout adheres to a meticulous order that guarantees every stage is built correctly on top of the last.

Phase 1: AI-Powered Student Support

- Chatbots for FAQs
- Microlearning tools
- Tutoring assistant

In this early stage, AI functions as scaffolding for readiness. Chatbots and FAQ tools reduce barriers by answering common questions, while microlearning modules introduce key coaching concepts. A tutoring assistant can provide additional reinforcement for participants who need more preparation. These supports do not replace human coaches but create psychological safety and orientation before coaching begins.

Phase 2: Coach Augmentation Tools

- Journaling prompts
- Reflective AI notes

- Session enhancements

Here, AI supports reflection and coaching practice between sessions. Journaling prompts, enriched by AI feedback, help clients recognize themes in their own words. Reflective AI notes can highlight recurring language or emotional cues, while session enhancements reduce administrative burdens for coaches. Coaches remain the interpreters, using AI signals as mirrors for deeper meaning rather than directives.

Phase 3: Coaching Analytics (with Consent)

- Time-on-task
- Consent-based data
- Trend analysis

With explicit client consent, anonymized data can be aggregated to analyze patterns such as time spent on tasks or recurring themes across cohorts. Trend analysis provides organizations with system-level insights while maintaining individual confidentiality. Bias auditing and strong consent protocols are essential: analytics should inform growth, not dictate or stereotype it.

Phase 4: Coach Training + AI Ethics Modules

- AI literacy programs
- Ethical frameworks
- Professional development

As AI becomes more integrated, coaches must be trained to use it responsibly. This includes AI literacy programs, instruction in ethical frameworks, and professional development opportunities to practice with applied cases. Peer learning and ongoing supervision ensure that coaches can identify when technology supports growth and when it risks harm.

Phase 5: Enterprise Coaching Platforms

- Human + AI co-coaching
- Multi-agent systems
- Scalable solutions

The final phase envisions enterprise-level coaching platforms that extend access without losing humanity. Human + AI co-coaching expands capacity, multi-agent systems coordinate insights across large teams, and scalable solutions bring coaching to global populations. In practice, this could mean personalization at scale, real-time translation, and safeguards to ensure equitable access across regions and cultures.

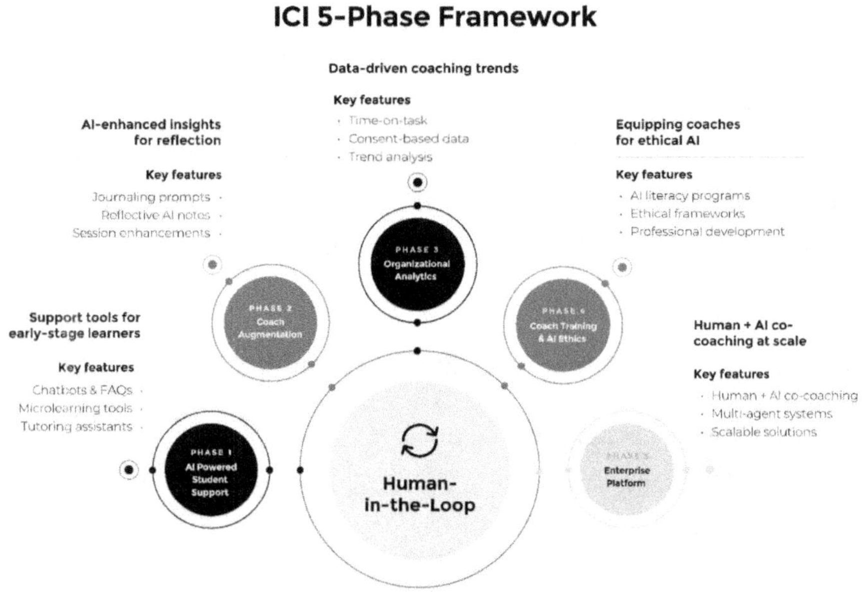

ICI 5-Phase Framework

Figure 5.3 The ICI 5-Phase Model

The ICI 5-phase model, first introduced in the white paper *Where AI Meets Empathy*^{TM}, represents this evolution as an integrated system in which each stage builds the groundwork for the next. At every stage, human discernment, presence, and empathy remain essential.

As one client expressed it: "The tool helped me name a pattern. But it was my coach who helped me face it."

This is the future of coaching: technology as scaffolding, human wisdom as foundation.

Illustrative Case: Scaling with Soul

Imagine a multinational healthcare organization seeking to provide coaching support to 15,000 healthcare workers in 12 nations, all of whom were suffering from burnout and moral distress in the aftermath of the global pandemic. Conventional coaching methods might reach possibly 200 individuals; they required an approach that had the capacity to scale and yet retain the depth and cultural sensitivity that healthcare workers deserved.

Applying the ICI 5-phase model as a design framework, the organization could proceed step by step:

Phase 1: Launch chatbots and FAQ tools to connect healthcare workers with resources, along with microlearning modules for resilience and tutoring assistants to orient participants to coaching. These supports reduce barriers and build readiness.

Phase 2: Introduce journaling prompts and reflective AI notes to help workers process challenging patient interactions with session enhancements that reduce administrative burden and free coaches to focus on presence.

Phase 3: With explicit consent, use time-on-task data and anonymized trend analysis to uncover shared stress patterns across roles, such as ICU nurses compared to emergency physicians or home healthcare workers, and tailor coaching accordingly.

Phase 4: Train an international coaching network with AI literacy programs, ethical frameworks, and professional development that integrates trauma-informed care and cultural responsiveness.

Phase 5: Deploy an enterprise coaching platform offering human + AI co-coaching, multi-agent systems to coordinate support, and scalable solutions to provide personalized, multilingual access. Scheduling, translation, and initial intake are handled by AI, while human coaches bring empathy, cultural intelligence, and clinical wisdom.

The result: a coaching system that is globally consistent and locally relevant, technologically sophisticated and deeply human.

This phased approach ensures technology supports rather than replaces the human elements of coaching. At every stage, ICI centers identity, context, and emotional intelligence as essential to responsible innovation.

Illustrative Example

To highlight the difference between an AI-only approach and AI guided by culturally responsive coaching, consider this simplified scenario of a global technology organization facing collaboration challenges across teams in different regions.

Scenario 1: AI-Only Approach

The organization uses an AI communication optimization platform, which examines email patterns, meeting interactions, and project communications. The system provides automated suggestions for every team member in order to enhance their "communication efficiency scores." Each week, team members are sent reports with recommended specific language changes and interaction patterns to align with algorithmic standards for effective collaboration.

Results: Though surface-level gains may appear, underlying cultural tensions remain unresolved. The Japanese team's relationship-centered, indirect style is flagged as inefficient, creating stress and frustration. Meanwhile, the U.S. team's direct, task-focused communication is rated as optimal, reinforcing imbalance rather than building understanding. Cultural richness is diminished when efficiency is defined only by algorithms.

Scenario 2: AI + Culturally Responsive Coaching

The same AI technology is introduced, but this time, coaches interpret the results through cultural and systemic lenses. Coaches work together with the team members to understand what the communication patterns reveal about work styles and cultural values. The technology provides data on interaction frequency and language use, while the coaches help translate those signals into collaborative practices that honor both cultural contexts.

Results: Team members gain deeper appreciation of cultural differences and develop practical strategies for collaboration. The AI results become tools for understanding instead of judgment, leading to innovations in project management that honor both efficiency and relationship-building. Trust increases both within and between teams.

The difference does not lie in the degree of technological advancement, but in whether human wisdom guides its application.

Summary: Where the Models Intersect

The ACI model protects the sacred space between coach and client.

The AIEC framework governs how organizations embed those same values within their cultures.

The ICI 5-phase model turns both into a living system that scales ethically and inclusively.

Together they form a complete ecosystem for human-centered innovation, an infrastructure designed not to replace empathy, but to expand its reach.

Chapter 5 Practice Lab

Practice Lab: Applying the ICI Frameworks

Activity 1: ACI in Action

Choose a client you are currently coaching, or create a hypothetical case. Apply the three pillars of the ACI Model—awareness, choice, integration—and map how you would use them in practice.

- Awareness: What would you explain about the AI tool? How transparent would you be about what the tool does, what data it uses, and what its limitations are?
- Choice: Where would you offer agency? Would the client opt in, opt out, or choose specific functions of the AI?
- Integration: How would you ensure the AI output supports the client's development goals rather than organizational metrics or your own convenience?

Write a short coaching dialogue that illustrates these choices. Notice where your human presence shapes the outcome.

Activity 2: AIEC Organizational Simulation

Imagine your organization is preparing to introduce AI into its leadership coaching program. Using the four AIEC pillars—awareness, integration, ethics, and collaboration—draft a framework for rollout.

- Awareness: What must leaders and participants know before adoption?
- Integration: How would you phase in the tools to reduce disruption?
- Ethics: What privacy, consent, and bias safeguards would be necessary?
- Collaboration: How would you involve participants as partners, not passive recipients?

Draft a one-page proposal or memo that outlines how these four pillars could structure a responsible adoption plan.

Activity 3: Scaling with the ICI 5-Phase Model

- Review the five phases of the ICI 5-phase model.
- For each phase:
    - Identify one benefit to clients if the phase is implemented well
    - Identify one risk if the phase is skipped or rushed
    - Suggest one feedback loop that would allow you to evaluate readiness before moving to the next phase

Visualize this as a construction schedule. Create a diagram or table showing how each phase builds upon the last, noting where ethical checkpoints are required before advancing.

Reflection Questions

- How do the ACI, AIEC, and ICI 5-phase models change the way you think about scaling AI in coaching?
- Reflect on whether you had previously considered AI integration as primarily a technical challenge.

- How does reframing it as an infrastructure of ethics, choice, and cultural responsiveness shift your perspective?
- Which pillar or phase feels most challenging to your current practice and why?
  - Consider whether it is awareness (understanding tools), choice (giving clients agency), ethics (privacy and bias safeguards), or integration (balancing human and AI inputs). Write about what makes this area difficult for you and how you might strengthen it.
- What would it take for your organization to strengthen its coaching infrastructure?
- Imagine your organization beginning to apply these models. What new roles, policies, or practices would need to be in place for AI to support, rather than undermine, trust and presence?
- If you were to teach these frameworks to another coach or leader, where would you begin?
- Draft a short teaching outline in your notes. What examples, metaphors, or case studies would you use to show why human discernment must guide technology?
- Looking ahead, how can you ensure technology remains a supporting scaffold rather than the primary structure of the coaching relationship?
- Identify two or three practical commitments you want to make. For example, "I will always discuss consent first," or "I will treat AI outputs as prompts, not prescriptions."

Moving Forward

The three frameworks outlined in this chapter are the architectural blueprints for the integration of ethical AI in coaching. Blueprints, however, only become buildings through expert implementation, meticulous attention to detail, and constant maintenance. ACI ensures that one-on-one coaching relationships retain their vital human components while leveraging the benefits of technology. AIEC supplies an organizational framework for AI integration at scale without quality loss or cultural sensitivity compromise. The 5-phase model gives a workable blueprint for progressing from pilot initiatives to company-wide execution.

Together, these frameworks address the root challenge of our time: How do we optimize the promise of artificial intelligence while protecting and amplifying what is most human in us? The success of any AI integration initiative depends not on the sophistication of the technology, but on the wisdom with which it's implemented. These frameworks provide that wisdom: distilled from years of field experience, refined through diverse cultural contexts, and grounded in the conviction that coaching's greatest value lies in its capacity to honor human complexity while facilitating transformation.

As we move into Chapter 6, we will examine what these frameworks actually sound like on a moment-to-moment basis. When AI enters the coaching room, literally or figuratively, how do coaches make the moment-to-moment decisions that will cause technology to enhance, not detract from, the coaching experience? The frameworks provide the structure; the next chapter is about the art of bringing them to life in real coaching conversation. The groundwork is firm. The designs are transparent. Now the task is to construct coaching infrastructure that not only integrates AI, but also supports human thriving in the era of artificial intelligence.

When AI Enters the Coaching Room

Jordan Kim, a Korean marketing manager at a Fortune 500 company, was intrigued by his new AI-powered coaching app. The tool promised real-time prompts during meetings. It suggested phrases to use, reminders to "speak with confidence," even gave tips on managing tone.

When he met with his coach, Jordan proudly pulled up the app. "It says I should use this phrase when I'm challenged: 'I appreciate your perspective, but here's where I stand.'"

He laughed nervously. "Honestly, it feels like having training wheels for leadership."

But as the weeks went on, Jordan grew uneasy. In one meeting, he followed a prompt word for word. Instead of sounding confident, he felt like a bad actor reading from a script. His colleagues seemed puzzled.

In his next coaching session, he blurted out, "I'm starting to feel like I'm performing for the AI, not leading my team. What if I can't do this without it?"

His coach didn't correct him or dismiss the concern. She let the silence stretch before asking, "What feels different when the words are yours?"

Jordan thought back. "When I speak in my own way, I connect better. People lean in. Even if I stumble, they know it's real."

The coach nodded. "So what if the AI is a mirror, not a script? A tool for reflection, not a substitute for your voice?"

The shift was subtle but profound. Jordan began using the app differently. Instead of parroting the prompts, he used them as practice material before meetings, as inspiration, not instruction. In the room, he relied on his own words.

A month later, he told his coach, "The AI helped me prepare. But when I spoke as myself, that's when my team trusted me."

The machine offered phrases. Coaching gave him permission to lead with authenticity.

* * *

You're leading a coaching session on Zoom.

Your client has just uploaded their journaling log from a generative AI app.

You've reviewed a dashboard of emotional tone trends over the last six weeks.

And your client begins by saying:

"The AI app generated a report suggesting I avoid feedback. What do you think?"

Welcome to the future of coaching, where AI is no longer a behind-the-scenes tool. It's in the room with us. The principles of awareness, choice, and integration become real-time practices at this moment.

This chapter examines the intersection of AI and coaching in real time, and how coaches can navigate this new terrain with integrity, empathy, and excellence.

The Rise of AI-Augmented Coaching

The infrastructure of coaching is evolving rapidly. As urban areas implement smart traffic systems that provide real-time feedback to streamline the flow of transportation, coaching practices are adopting AI tools that provide continuous feedback on client patterns, growth, and needs. But whereas traffic flow systems can be reduced to algorithms, coaching infrastructure must be capable of embracing the entire spectrum of human development, including cultural identity, emotional depth, and systemic context that algorithms are prone to miss.

Across the field, coaches are experimenting with AI to support the coaching process in areas such as:

- Pre-session preparation
  - Summaries of previous sessions and client journals
  - Mood monitoring and goal diaries
  - AI-assisted orientation and readiness prompts
- In-session augmentation
  - Real-time reflection prompts and emotion parsing
  - Dynamic questioning based on client responses
  - Sentiment analysis during virtual sessions
  - Identification of cultural communication styles
  - Alerts for bias in coach language and assumptions
- Post-session integration
  - Session recaps and progress tracking across multiple goals
  - Personalized reflection questions based on session material
  - Practice suggestions aligned with client learning styles
  - Integration exercises that connect one session to the next

These applications do not replace the coach. They expand the coaching experience when used with intentionality. But thoughtful use requires clear models, strong boundaries, and ethical guidelines, ones that keep human infrastructure as the primary system being supported. That is why the principles of the ACI and AIEC frameworks, together with the ICI 5-phase model, are so critical: they ensure AI tools enhance coaching without overshadowing the human relationship.

Real Coaching Scenarios and How to Navigate Them

The key to successful AI integration is to keep the coach in control of interpretation while leveraging AI for deeper insight. Below are common situations coaches encounter, and methods that ensure human wisdom remains the primary interpretive system:

Scenario: AI Surfaces a Blind Spot

The AI system generates an observation suggesting the client may avoid conflict.

Coach Response:

> "Let's explore what that means for you. When you read that, what was your first reaction? How does that line up with your experience?"

Why this works: The coach uses the AI output as an entry point for client self-discovery rather than adopting it as diagnostic truth. This aligns with the ACI pillar of integration, ensuring that technology supports the client's self-discovery.

Scenario: AI Suggests an Action Plan

The system produces a set of recommended next steps.

Coach Response:

"Those are interesting suggestions. Before we look at them, what feels most urgent or meaningful for you right now?"

Why this works: Client agency drives the agenda. This reflects the ACI pillar of choice, where AI recommendations are considered options, not directives.

Scenario: The Organization Reviews AI Data

The client is concerned that their AI-derived insights are being monitored by their manager.

Coach Response:

"Your privacy matters. Let's clarify what's shared, what isn't, and what choices you have. You get to lead this process."

Why This Works: The coach reinforces ethics and awareness (AIEC pillars), maintaining trust by clarifying boundaries and ensuring transparency.

Scenario: Cultural Misinterpretation

An AI app flags a client's communication style as passive when it is conveying cultural norms of respect and hierarchy.

Coach Response:

"The system is picking up on patterns in your communication. Let's talk about how your cultural background shapes your leadership style and the strengths you bring to your work."

Why this works: The coach retranslates AI results through a culturally responsive lens, affirming identity while fostering growth. This ties to both integration (ACI) and collaboration (AIEC).

Scenario: AI Overwhelm

Scenario: A client becomes preoccupied with maximizing their AI-generated scores instead of focusing on real development.

Coach Response:

"I notice you're working hard on the metrics. What would leadership development look like for you if we didn't have any of these measures?"

Why this works: The coach redirects attention from algorithmic optimization to intrinsic motivation and authentic development goals.

Illustrative Case:
Phase 2 – Reclaiming Voice Through Reflection

Title: *Finding Her Voice in a Room Full of Noise*

Challenge:

A mid-career finance executive, praised for her precision and analysis, struggled to be heard in senior leadership meetings. Surrounded by louder, more aggressive peers, she frequently softened her contributions to avoid conflict. Even when her expertise was decisive, she deferred to others, creating a pattern of invisibility that undermined her growing reputation.

Context:

The environment was high-stakes and fast-moving, where debate often rewarded volume over nuance. Her coaching intake revealed a leader who was exhausted from self-censorship, quietly questioning whether her collaborative style had a place at the executive table.

Coaching Engagement (Illustrative Scenario):

Using reflective AI notes and session enhancements aligned with Phase 2 of the ICI 5-phase model, the coach identified recurring patterns in her client's language: frequent disclaimers ("I might be wrong, but…"), apologetic qualifiers, and indirect phrasing during discussions of risk. With consent, these AI-supported insights shaped journaling prompts around decision ownership, setting boundaries, and reauthoring her leadership identity.

Transformation:

The leader began testing small but deliberate changes: making declarative statements about financial forecasts, asking clarifying questions without apology, and offering direct feedback to peers. Reviewing reflective AI notes, she remarked: "It surprised me to see how often I diluted my own expertise. Having those words reflected helped me step into my authority."

Architectural Framework:

- Clear foundations: Trust and cultural awareness were established first. The coach explored how gender norms in finance had shaped her communication style, ensuring safety for honest self-reflection.

- Proper scaffolding: AI provided scaffolding through pattern recognition and session notes, offering support but never dictating conclusions.

- Structural integrity: Ethical safeguards were present throughout consent, client control over what data to use, and confidentiality of reflective records.

- Successful outcome: The result was a leader who could hold authority without abandoning her collaborative nature. Her voice became both strategic and authentic, allowing her to influence more effectively in senior forums.

Link to ICI Phase 2:

This scenario illustrates how coach augmentation tools enrich coaching. By surfacing invisible language patterns and reinforcing client reflection, AI acted as scaffolding, but the real transformation came from the coaching relationship that enabled the business leader to reclaim authority on her own terms.

Illustrative Example

Let's examine how the same leadership voice challenge might unfold under different approaches:

Scenario 1: AI-Only Approach

An organization adopts an AI communications platform that tracks employee interactions and provides automated feedback on leadership presence. The system flags the mid-career leader for excessive apologetic language and low assertiveness scores. She receives weekly AI-generated reports with specific phrase replacements and assertiveness training modules. Progress is tracked through continuous language analysis.

Results: While her speech becomes more direct, she loses her natural collaborative strengths. Team members remark that she seems less approachable, and her attempts to follow AI's prescriptions come across as inauthentic. The optimization process strips away cultural and personal elements that once made her leadership effective.

Scenario 2: AI + Culturally Responsive Coaching

The same AI tools highlight communication patterns, but this time a coach interprets them within cultural and organizational context. Together, client and coach examine how gender dynamics, organizational culture, and individual values shape the client's communication. The AI provides signals about language use, but the coach helps her decide when to apply different strategies.

Results: The leader cultivates sophisticated communication skills that respect both her natural style and her development aspirations. She becomes intentional about code-switching, speaking collaboratively when consensus-building and speaking directly when her expertise must be understood clearly. Her team finds her both more confident and more authentically herself. The AI feedback offers tools for awareness, not directives for optimization.

The distinction is whether technology is employed to homogenize human behavior or to enhance human choice and self-knowledge.

The Infrastructure Challenge: Preserving Human Control

When AI comes into the coaching space, it can quietly change the balance of power in the relationship. Clients may start to favor algorithmic answers over their own inner knowledge. Coaches may feel compelled to justify their worth over machine effectiveness. Organizations may prioritize AI metrics over human growth.

Keeping the infrastructure healthy involves ensuring that coaches continue to be the chief meaning-makers while using AI as an advanced tool for pattern identification and insight generation. This involves:

- Establishing clear foundations:
    - Client self-knowledge takes precedence over AI analysis
    - Coach cultural and contextual awareness guides interpretation of all data

- Human relationships remain the primary tools of transformation
  - AI provides information; humans provide meaning
- Setting protective boundaries:
  - Clients maintain control over which AI insights to explore
  - Privacy protocols block AI data from being utilized for performance measurement
  - Cultural context determines the meaning of AI-flagged patterns
  - Coaches retain the authority to bypass AI suggestions when human insight indicates otherwise
- Developing interpretive capacity:
  - Coaches build competencies in identifying AI limitations and bias
  - Customers are taught to critically assess AI-driven insights instead of taking them as fact
  - Cultural responsiveness models guide all AI interpretations
  - Systemic awareness teaches understanding of individual patterns

These practices echo the principles of awareness, choice, and integration from the ACI model, and extend into organizational guardrails through the AIEC framework. Together, they ensure AI enhances human wisdom instead of displacing it.

Chapter 6 Practice Lab:
Coaching in Real Time with AI

Activity 1: AI Scenario Planning

Imagine you are exploring three AI tools in your coaching practice (for example: transcription assistants, reflective journaling apps, or mood-tracking dashboards). For each tool, create response scripts for common scenarios you may encounter:

- When AI uncovers insights that contradict your coaching instinct:

  How will you acknowledge the AI observation while upholding your professional discernment? What questions will you ask to help the client evaluate AI insights critically, without outsourcing their self-knowledge?

- When clients become too focused on AI metrics:

  How will you redirect attention back to intrinsic motivation and authentic development? What language will help you reframe AI data as information to consider, not instructions to obey?

- When AI suggestions appear culturally insensitive:

  How will you address potential bias without dismissing the technology entirely? What process will you use to surface cultural context that the AI may have overlooked?

Activity 2: Presence Practice in AI-Augmented Sessions

Coaching presence is tested when AI enters the session. Create a personal protocol for maintaining presence before, during, and after sessions where AI tools are engaged.

- Before the session:

  How will you review AI-generated insights critically without letting them bias your listening? What practices will keep you fully available to what arises in the moment?

- During the session:

  How will you balance attention to AI data with attention to the client's lived experience? What cues will remind you to prioritize the human relationship over technological efficiency?

- After the session:

  How will you integrate AI results with your observations and intuition? What reflection practices will help you evaluate whether the AI tools were helpful, neutral, or distracting?

Activity 3: Integration of Cultural Context

Cultural responsiveness remains essential when AI is used to analyze client patterns. Select a recent coaching scenario, real or imagined, where AI tools presented insights about a client's behaviors or communication style. Reflect and respond:

- Analyze the AI interpretation:

  What cultural assumptions might be embedded in the AI's analysis? How might the client's identity (race, gender, culture, or generation) influence the meaning of these patterns? What systemic issues could the AI be overlooking?

- Develop culturally responsive questions:

  What questions would invite the client to explore the cultural context of their patterns? How would you affirm their identity while pursuing growth opportunities? What alternatives to AI recommendations might better support this client's development?

- Practice integration:

How would you present AI results in a way that invites curiosity rather than compliance? What language would empower the client to maintain ownership of their development process?

Reflection Questions

- Balancing instinct and analysis:

When an AI tool generates an insight that does not align with your own instincts, how do you respond? What principles guide you in mediating conflicts between algorithmic analysis and your human discernment?

- Coaching presence in the moment:

Reflect on how your sense of presence shifts when AI tools are engaged during sessions. Do you feel distracted, biased, or more attuned? What practices might help you return to the client, even when technology is in the room?

- Protecting client agency:

AI-generated insights can appear more objective than human observation. How do you ensure that clients remain in charge of meaning-making and do not outsource authority to the algorithm?

- Cultural lenses and AI:

Consider the cultural factors in your own background that influence how you interpret client behavior. How might your perspective differ from the assumptions embedded in AI training data? What risks arise when cultural nuance is flattened into generic patterns?

- When AI helps, and when it hinders:

  Think of a situation where AI tools facilitated coach–client connection, and one where they created obstacles. What distinguished the two? How can you recognize those conditions in advance?

- Privacy and power:

  How do you address client concerns about surveillance or organizational misuse of AI-derived data? What language and boundaries strengthen trust in these conversations?

- Trusting the tools without losing humanity:

  What conditions—safeguards, training, or ethical guidelines— would you need to feel comfortable integrating AI tools into your practice while protecting the depth and authenticity of the human relationship?

Moving Forward

Throughout this chapter, we have explored the daily realities of coaching when AI enters the room: literally in the form of apps and screens, or metaphorically in the form of patterns and insights that it makes visible. The key to successful integration lies not in choosing between human intuition and artificial intelligence, but in choreographing their collaboration with expertise, intention, and cultural awareness.

The infrastructure metaphor also calls to mind that successful AI integration requires sound human systems to guide, interpret, and contextualize technological possibilities. In the same way that a city's electrical infrastructure brings power to buildings but requires human engineers to design safe distribution systems, AI coaching platforms bring data and insights that require human coaches to implement safely and effectively. The scenarios and recommendations outlined above provide pragmatic solutions for ensuring coaching efficacy while harnessing AI potential. Yet they also suggest more fundamental questions regarding authority, agency, and authenticity in helping relationships.

As technologies become more sophisticated and more ubiquitous, coaches must become equally adept at protecting human depth while welcoming technological augmentation. The illustrative case of reclaiming voice through AI-supported reflection shows what is possible when technology serves human development rather than dictating it. The person in that illustrative case did not shape herself to meet an algorithm's standards; she used AI insights as mirrors for deeper self-reflection and choice.

This model is the future of coaching: not human versus artificial intelligence, but human wisdom guiding AI capability. Not efficiency versus empathy, but efficiency in service of empathy. Not standardization versus personalization, but technology that enables more nuanced personalization.

As we transition into Chapter 7, we turn to the challenge of scale. How can the human depth and cultural sensitivity we've emphasized here be preserved when coaching expands across cultures and organizations? How can relational closeness endure as programs grow in size and complexity? The answers lie in designing infrastructure that is both technologically advanced and profoundly human. But scale also brings scrutiny: the larger the program, the greater the demand to prove it works. That is where we now turn, to the challenge of measurement in a hybrid coaching world.

Scaling Without Sacrificing Humanity

Carmen Rodriguez had spent fifteen years cultivating her reputation as one of the pharmaceutical industry's most popular executive coaches. The founder of a boutique firm specializing in leadership coaching for life sciences, she and her small team worked with C-suite executives on three continents, and her calendar was always booked months in advance.

When the world's largest client for her firm came to talk to her about implementing expanded coaching services to 500 middle managers across their worldwide operations, Carmen felt both thrilled and intimidated.

"Five hundred people, Carmen," said her fellow faculty coach, Anthony Marcus, during lunch. "That's phenomenal growth for your business."

Carmen whirled the coffee in her cup slowly. "That's exactly what scares me. How do I scale what I do without losing the secret sauce that makes it successful? My clients trust me because I understand them. I recall their stories, their problems, their growth edges. How do I duplicate that level of intimacy with hundreds of people?"

"What if scaling doesn't mean watering down how you do things," said Anthony, who had recently completed advanced training on integrating AI tools into coaching practice. "What if it means amplifying it?"

Carmen raised an eyebrow. "I don't understand."

"Think back on the following," Anthony said. "You already keep notes on client progress. You already recognize language and behavior patterns with clients. You already individualize how you go about things with their culture and communication style. What if there are ways that AI could help you systematize all of that across a coaching team, so you could maintain the focus on doing things that only you can do? AI can also take on pre-work, homework prompts, and session summaries for managers freeing you and your coaches to stay present."

Carmen was unimpressed. "But coaching isn't about systems. It's about relationships."

"Exactly. And relationships are built on understanding, consistency, and presence. AI can help you maintain that understanding across more people. It can help you spot patterns you might miss when you're juggling so many clients. It can help you prepare for sessions more effectively. But it can't replace your presence, your intuition, or your ability to hold space for transformation."

Over the following months, Carmen worked with Anthony to design a scaled coaching program that preserved her relational approach while strategically leveraging technology. She discovered that AI tools could enhance her ability to track themes across her growing client base, generate culturally responsive reflection prompts between sessions, deliver pre-work and homework to managers, and maintain continuity through session summary notes even when scheduling conflicts arose.

Six months later, Carmen told Anthony, "I was afraid that scaling would mean losing the human connection. Instead, I found that thoughtful use of technology actually helped me be more human with each client. The AI handles the data so I can focus entirely on the person sitting across from me."

Carmen's experience illustrates a fundamental truth about human infrastructure in the AI age: scaling doesn't require sacrificing depth. When properly designed, technological systems can strengthen the human foundation rather than replace it. The key lies in understanding which elements need human attention and which can be enhanced through artificial intelligence.

* * *

In the same way that cities build architectural infrastructure to connect communities rather than isolate them, coaches can use AI infrastructure to extend their reach while deepening their impact. The scaffold systems that hold this work in place will need to be constructed with the same thoughtfulness and forethought that would go into any critical construction endeavor.

How Coaches Can Leverage AI Tools Ethically

Consider the rise of tools that:

- Transcribe and analyze sessions
- Offer sentiment tracking or tone analysis
- Provide feedback on the coach's language usage
- Suggest personalized resources based on client goals
- Deliver pre-work, homework, and reflection prompts between sessions
- Generate session summary notes for continuity

Used appropriately, these tools:

- Increase reflection depth
- Accelerate insight
- Support accountability

- Reveal coaching blind spots

Used carelessly, they:

- Invade privacy
- Erode trust
- Risk over-reliance on machine judgment

The architectural metaphor assists us in grasping this balance. Transport networks function best when they take people to places that are relevant to them, not when they decide where people ought to go. In the same way, tools for AI coaching function best when they bring coaches and clients together with insights relevant to their development objectives, not when they enforce pre-determined ends. Crafting successful coaching infrastructure depends on an awareness of the difference between facilitating human connection and replacing it. AI is capable of offering the structure that unites the relationships of the coach over space and time, but the quality of the structure rests exclusively on the caliber of the human connections it facilitates.

Ethical Guardrails

As introduced in Chapter 4, ethical guardrails remain essential whenever AI enters the coaching process. At scale, they become even more critical. These guardrails function as scaffolding systems that ensure safety and stability across large coaching infrastructures:

- Informed consent – Clients must understand what data is used, stored, and analyzed
- Data minimization – Only necessary insights should be used, and only for coaching
- Bias awareness – Coaches must be able to spot and challenge algorithmic bias

- Cultural humility – AI may miss identity-based context; coaches must not

These ethical guidelines act as systems of scaffolding that provide safe integration of AI through the whole coaching infrastructure. Each element has its unique structural function in upholding the integrity of the human-centered approach:

- Consent protocols act as safety railings that guard clients against falling into monitoring or data exploitation. Just as construction areas need barriers to keep workers away from unsafe zones, data collection needs explicit boundaries set around the use. These protocols aren't delays; they ensure the whole process is safer for all parties involved.

- Data minimization acts as structural load limits that keep the infrastructure from becoming overtaxed with extraneous information. Engineers determine how much weight the bridge ought to hold; coaches need to determine how much data supports client development versus organizational expediency. Gathering information relevant to development alone keeps the focus on change rather than monitoring.

- Bias awareness functions as alignment and leveling checks, the equivalent of plumb lines, tolerance testing, and periodic structural surveys to make sure the system stays true. Regular bias audits, red-team reviews, and escalation paths for challenging outputs prevent hidden lean or drift in the structure and reduce the risk of replicating inequities at scale.

- Cultural humility is like a foundation inspection that ensures the foundational support structures remains stable across varying populations. Buildings need frequent stress points identified through inspection before they are at risk of structural collapse. Coach programs need frequent culture audits to identify where the AI systems are possibly misinterpreting identity-based communication patterns or perpetuating established biases.

The ACI model offers architectural blueprints for ethical AI use in individual coaching engagements that can be applied across varying settings with structural integrity. As introduced in Chapter 5, the ACI model centers on three pillars—awareness, choice, integration—so coaches and clients stay aware of what AI is doing, clients retain genuine choice (including opting out), and AI is integrated only when it advances the client's goals within their cultural and organizational context.

Each system of scaffolding brings its part to the strategy to develop an infrastructure that can scale without losing safety or efficacy. They give the structural support needed for scaling human-centered coaching in the world of technology-extended human abilities.

Consent, Transparency, and Co-Creation

Before using AI-enhanced coaching tools, three principles must guide the process:

1. Informed Consent

Clients must understand how the tool works, what data is collected, and where that data is stored. No coaching innovation is worth breaching trust.

2. Transparency

Be clear when you're using AI. Don't let it run silently in the background. It's not a secret weapon; it's a shared partner.

3. Co-Creation

Involve the client in deciding which tools to use, how to interpret the results, and what insights are most important. Coaching with AI should still be coaching *with* the client.

These three principles mirror the ethical guidelines outlined in ICI's AI ethics toolkit, ensuring that technology never overrides human choice, consent, or cultural context. By anchoring practice in consent, transparency, and co-creation, coaches maintain trust while responsibly integrating AI at scale.

Illustrative Case:
Phase 3 – Organizational Coaching Analytics

Illustrative Case: *Coaching Where the Risks Are Real*

Challenge:
Two leaders in high-stakes roles, one in safety, one in cybersecurity, were under pressure to prove value while facing systemic bias and limited psychological safety.

Approach:
Organizational coaching analytics (Phase 3) revealed anonymized patterns (e.g., self-minimizing language, over-indexing on others' needs) that might otherwise have remained invisible at scale. Coaches then interpreted those patterns with identity and context in mind.

Outcome:
Leaders reframed their communication styles and strengthened advocacy, influence, and self-trust. "I've learned to listen more closely, not just to others, but to myself."

Link to Model:

This example illustrates how Phase 3 can reveal equity-relevant insights while keeping humans in the loop for interpretation and care.

Illustrative Case:
Phase 5 – Enterprise Coaching Platforms

Illustrative Case: *The Co-Coaching Platform That Made Coaching Scalable and Personal*

Challenge:

A global infrastructure company wanted to expand coaching access to over 400 emerging leaders across five continents without turning coaching into a checkbox.

Program Design:

An enterprise coaching platform (Phase 5) combines human coaching with AI-powered tools. Between sessions, participants receive AI-assisted journaling prompts, coach-reviewed summaries, and optional multilingual micro-lessons on coaching themes (e.g., boundary-setting, courage, trust). Anonymous trend tracking helps learning and development teams notice patterns (e.g., burnout, communication tension) without exposing individual data.

Architectural View:

- Foundations: Cultural awareness and trust-building across time zones, languages, and diverse concepts of feedback/vulnerability
- Scaffolding: Pre-work, homework, and summaries to support continuity
- Structural integrity: Ethical guardrails and privacy protections
- Completion: Expanded access without loss of human connection

Link to ICI Phase 5:

Link to ICI Phase 5: This scenario brings to life how humans and technology can partner to deliver coaching that's expansive, accessible, and emotionally intelligent at scale.

Illustrative Example

In order to clarify the distinction between AI solutions alone and AI-supplemented empathetic coaching, let us examine the above-cited scenario with the world infrastructure company using two different approaches:

Scenario 1: AI-Only Approach

The company deploys an overall AI-based coaching platform that supplies all 400 future leaders with personalized automated development plans through initial assessments. The platform offers weekly check-ins, tracking, adjustments to goals, and resource alignments. Members primarily deal with chatbots and get automated constructive feedback according to their input on standardized questions.

Leaders complete monthly surveys about their progress, and the AI generates performance reports for managers. The platform tracks completion rates, engagement metrics, and goal achievement across the global population. Participants who fall behind receive automated encouragement messages and additional resource recommendations.

Results: Although the platform excels with high efficacy and uniform delivery on all continents, participants feel distanced from the growth process. Most report the experience as an exercise in going through the motions but not actual growth. Cultural subtleties are lost, individual issues are missed, and retention percentages fall with leaders losing enthusiasm through the absence of human connection.

The same organization implements an AI-enhanced coaching platform that pairs each of the 400 leaders with human coaches supported by intelligent tools. The AI provides coaches with cultural context, language preferences, and development themes for each participant. Between human coaching sessions, participants receive personalized pre-work, homework between sessions, reflection prompts curated by their coaches using AI insights.

Coaches use AI-generated summaries to maintain continuity across sessions and identify patterns that might otherwise be missed across such a large population. The platform tracks anonymous trends that help organizational leaders understand systemic challenges while preserving individual privacy. Human coaches remain the primary relationship for each participant, with AI serving as an enhancement tool.

Results: Participants exhibit greater satisfaction, deeper connections with coaches, and better development relevance. Human empathy combined with the efficiency of AI results in scalable coaching infrastructure with no loss of human focus. Retention goes up, and participants show observable growth in technical skills as well as leadership presence.

The distinction is not in the refinement of the technology itself, but in how human prudence informs its application. The approach with artificial intelligence acknowledges that scaling is not about replacing human relationships but fortifying human connections.

Chapter 7 Practice Lab

Activity 1: Scaling Assessment

Evaluate your current coaching practice or leadership development approach using the infrastructure framework:

Boundary Assessment:

- Identify three fundamental values that steer your relationships as a coach
- Which among these values would be compromised by rapid scaling?
- Explain how you will maintain these values when expanding outreach

Designing Scaffolding:

- Choose three AI tools that could support your coaching without replacing human connection
- For each tool, write one sentence describing how it fills in or complements rather than replaces your approach
- Identify potential risks of each tool and design safeguards to mitigate them

Load Testing:

- Work through your present capability (number of clients, sessions per week, prep time)
- Estimate how AI tools could increase your effective capacity while maintaining quality
- Create a pilot program for piloting scaled coaching with three to five additional clients

Activity 2: Ethical Guardrails Design

Develop an inclusive ethical foundation for AI-facilitated coaching in your situation:

Consent Protocol Building:

- Draft a client consent form that explains AI use in simple, accessible language

- Include specific examples of what data will and will not be collected
- Create an opt-out process that maintains coaching effectiveness without AI tools

Theoretical Orientations Review:

- Identify five ways in which AI tools may misconstrue cultural communication behavior
- Design questions you would ask to understand the cultural context for each client
- Create an objection process for challenging AI recommendations that are culturally insensitive

Bias Identification Practice:

- Investigate the training data for three tools that you would apply when coaching
- Recognize potential biases in each tool according to its training data
- Make a list for identifying when outputs by AI may indicate prejudice instead of perception

Activity 3: Scale Planning Workshop

Create an acceleration plan for the coaching services that preserves human touch:

Infrastructure Mapping:

- Create a diagram illustrating how human relationships with coaches would be facilitated by tools with AI functionality
- Include clear boundaries between AI functions and human responsibilities

- Demonstrate how data flows between individual components yet keeps information private

Pilot Design:

- Create 90-day pilot program for scaled coaching with clear success metrics
- Include both quantitative indicators (retention, satisfaction, goal accomplishment) and qualitative measures (depth of relationship, cultural competence, transformation narratives)
- Schedule frequent check-ins to determine if scaling is fortifying or dismantling coaching relationships

Sustainability Planning:

- Calculate the resources required to maintain quality as coaching services expand
- Point out where human infrastructure would likely be stress points
- Design early warning systems that alert you when scaling is compromising coaching effectiveness

Reflection Questions

Personal Practice Reflection

- Which part of your approach to coaching would you never automate, no matter how technology has advanced?
- How do you maintain current strong relationships with clients, and how could these procedures be enhanced through the assistance of AI?
- What are your concerns when thinking of expanding your business as a coach, and how would judicious integration with AI reduce rather than increase these fears?

Ethical Issues

- How do you balance client confidentiality with organizational value for aggregated insights on coaching?
- What cultural variables in your own heritage could impact your interpretation of data generated by an AI coach?
- When AI tools suggest interpretations that conflict with your coaching intuition, what process do you use to determine which perspective to trust?

Systemic Impact

- In what ways could AI-enriched coaching impact power relations among the communities you represent?
- What responsibility do coaches have for ensuring AI tools don't perpetuate existing inequities in leadership development?
- How can scaled coach programs assist rather than disrupt diversity and inclusion in organizational leadership?

Future Preparation

- What emerging skills will coaches develop with increasingly advanced and pervasive AI tools?
- How will you further hone your coaching skills as AI picks up increasing routine coaching responsibilities?
- What is the place of human coaches in teaching AI systems how to better reach diverse populations?

Quality Assurance

- How do you measure the depth and authenticity of coaching relationships when technology mediates more interactions?
- What indicators suggest that AI integration is enhancing rather than replacing human connection in coaching?

- How frequently must the coaching infrastructure be reviewed for ethical adherence and cultural sensibility?

Looking Ahead

This chapter has explored how coaching can expand its reach while maintaining its essential humanity. The infrastructure metaphor reveals that successful scaling requires building strong foundations, implementing proper scaffolding, and maintaining structural integrity throughout the growth process.

The cases and frameworks presented here demonstrate that scale and depth are not opposing forces. When AI integration is guided by ethical principles and cultural responsiveness, technology can actually strengthen human connections rather than replace them. The key lies in understanding which elements of coaching require human presence and which can be enhanced through artificial intelligence.

The story of Carmen, with which we began this chapter, illustrates the potential for transformation when coaches treat scale as the possibility to expand human impact rather than scale out of it. In Carmen's example, the integration of thoughtful AI doesn't diminish the relational richness that is key to the transformational power of coaching but rather lets the coach scale to reach additional people.

The systems in this chapter—consent protocols, data minimization practices, bias awareness, cultural audits, and ethical standards—offer the structural bearings needed to develop effective diversity-serving coaching infrastructure. They help ensure expansion fortifies, rather than undermines, the humanity in the practice of coaching.

As the profession evolves further in the age of artificial intelligence, its challenge will be balancing this integration of efficacy with compassion, standardization with individualization, and scaling up with cultural sensitivity. These models and practices guide the evolution, but the process will require ongoing vigilance and responsiveness.

The following chapter explores how we quantify success in this world of hybrid coaching. If human wisdom and artificial intelligence coauthor the results of coaching, how do we determine the efficacy? What indicators register the transmutation without commodifying the human beings as data points? How do we judge the wellness of the coaching ecosystem with all due respect for the richness of human growth?

These questions become more pressing as coaching programs scale and stakeholders demand evidence of return on investment. The challenge lies in creating measurement systems that provide accountability without undermining the trust and vulnerability that make coaching transformational.

Chapter 8 explores how coaches and organizations can navigate this complex terrain while preserving the humanity that makes coaching essential in the AI age.

What Gets Measured in a Hybrid Coaching World

Dr. Sarah Chen stared at the dashboard on her screen, feeling increasingly frustrated. As the head of leadership development for a global consulting firm, she had championed the implementation of an AI-enhanced coaching program six months earlier.

The numbers looked impressive: 89% goal completion rate, 4.2 average satisfaction score, 127% increase in session frequency. Her executive team was pleased with the data-driven results. But Sarah felt something was missing.

Over coffee with her long-time mentor, Dr. James Thompson, an organizational psychologist with decades of experience, she voiced her unease. As always, their conversation focused on program design and de-identified insights, keeping all client information strictly confidential.

"The metrics look great on paper," Sarah said. "But I'm not convinced we're actually measuring what matters. Are we tracking transformation or just transactions?"

James leaned back. "What's bothering you about the numbers?"

"Well, I know from our coaching team that one of our high-potential Latina leaders is excelling according to the dashboard: high engagement scores, consistent journaling, hitting all her development milestones. But her coach also shared that she's struggling with belonging at her level. She's adapting constantly in meetings, code-switching to fit in, and the AI is labeling that as inauthentic. In reality, she's using a sophisticated survival strategy in environments that don't yet feel fully safe."

Sarah paused, then continued. "The AI is tracking her participation, but it's not showing us how much emotional energy she's spending to maintain that adaptation. Her high performance scores don't tell us whether her growth is sustainable, or if the system is pushing her to compromise parts of her identity just to succeed."

James nodded. "So how would meaningful measurement play out for her?"

"That's the challenge," Sarah admitted. "How do you measure identity integration? Or confidence to lead authentically when it's safe to do so? The AI will tell us she's achieving her goals, but it won't tell us if those goals are advancing her development in ways that matter to her."

James leaned forward. "Maybe the issue isn't how to measure it for her, but how to create space for her to measure it herself. What if the most relevant metrics are the ones she sets for her own development?"

In the weeks that followed, Sarah consulted with her coaching team about redesigning their approach to measurement. They kept the quantitative dashboards for organizational accountability but added co-measurement practices: quarterly conversations where clients reflected on their own indicators of progress alongside organizational measures.

Three months later, in aggregate feedback from her coaching team, Sarah noticed a shift in how clients described their own growth. One Latina leader, speaking in a voluntary reflection exercise, shared: "I used to think success meant leaving parts of me at the door. Now I understand that my adaptability is a strength, and I get to decide when and how to use it."

The dashboard still indicated steady participation, but Sarah knew there was a deeper narrative beneath the numbers: leadership that emerged not from erasing identity but from navigating complexity with agency.

"We're not just measuring what she does," Sarah reflected with James later. "We're creating space for her to understand why it matters."

* * *

Sarah's experience highlights a fundamental challenge in building human infrastructure for the AI age: the most important transformations often resist quantification. Like cities that measure traffic flow but struggle to capture community connection, coaching programs can track participation while missing the deeper work of identity development, cultural integration, and authentic leadership emergence.

The infrastructure metaphor reminds us that measurement systems must serve the people they're designed to support, not the other way around. Effective measurement infrastructure includes both the visible metrics that demonstrate accountability and the underlying support systems that honor human complexity.

In every coaching engagement, the question eventually comes up: "How do we know this is working?"

Organizations want ROI. Clients want to track progress. Coaches want to refine their craft.

Now, with AI in the mix, the pressure, and the possibility of measuring impact, is higher than ever.

But here's the challenge: What matters in coaching is often what's hardest to quantify.

Trust. Insight. Empathy. Transformation.

So, how do we balance meaningful measurement with human complexity?

The Metrics That Matter

Traditional coaching metrics often include:

- Goal achievement
- 360-degree feedback improvements
- Employee engagement scores
- Leadership pipeline advancement

With AI-augmented coaching, new metrics are emerging:

- Emotional tone shifts over time (via journaling or sentiment analysis)
- Coaching session patterns (e.g., frequency, pacing, focus areas)
- AI-logged goals vs. actual development themes
- Self-assessment trends prompted by AI reflections

These can offer valuable insight, but only when interpreted with caution and context.

Quantitative ≠ Transformational

AI can track what, but only the coach and client can interpret the why. For example:

- A spike in self-reported confidence might coincide with burnout denial
- Decreased journaling frequency might mean progress or disconnection

In a hybrid world, metrics must be paired with meaningful human reflection, which is why ICI's model prioritizes co-measurement, a process where the coach and client discuss:

- What does success look like?
- What feels different, not just what looks different?
- What should or shouldn't be tracked over time?

Illustrative Example:
Phase 3—Measuring What Matters Across Cultures

One example of how measurement can either distort or reveal meaning comes from a global bank that implemented AI-augmented coaching across regional offices.

Challenge:

The dashboards suggested leaders in Western Europe were more engaged than peers in Asia and Latin America. Executives assumed this meant some regions were less committed to leadership development.

Issue:

On paper, the data suggested disengagement. But coaches in Asia and Latin America noticed otherwise. Leaders were deeply engaged, they simply interacted differently. Some of them journal less often but with more depth. Others preferred group dialogue over individual surveys. The AI interpreted these differences as low participation, overlooking cultural norms around communication and reflection.

Approach:

Using organizational coaching analytics (Phase 3 of the ICI model), anonymized data was re-examined alongside coach insights. Metrics were redesigned to account for cultural context: reflection depth, communication style, and decision-making pace.

Outcome:

The bank shifted its evaluation from volume of contributions to quality and context of contributions. Leaders across regions felt their authentic engagement styles were respected, while executives gained awareness that Western norms were not universal.

Architectural view:

- Clear foundations: Respect for cultural differences in how leadership engagement is expressed
- Proper scaffolding: AI analytics paired with coach interpretation
- Structural integrity: Bias audits to prevent systemic mislabeling of cultural behaviors
- Successful completion: Metrics that honored authentic growth across all regions

This example shows how measurement infrastructure can either reinforce inequities or dismantle them, depending on whether AI-generated data is interpreted with cultural responsiveness.

A Culturally Responsive Approach to Data

Not all metrics are neutral. Bias can show up in:

- How performance is defined
- Who gets to decide what "growth" looks like
- Which data is considered valid

ICI trains coaches to ask:

- Whose metrics are these?
- What cultural assumptions shape them?
- How can we co-create measurements that center equity and identity?

For example, a Black woman navigating systemic bias may appear quiet in meetings, not from disengagement, but as a form of strategic self-preservation. An AI tool might flag this as low engagement. A culturally responsive coach interprets context before drawing conclusions.

As with the ethical guardrails introduced in Chapter 4, measurement systems also require scaffolding: consent protocols, cultural audits, and bias reviews to ensure data supports client development rather than organizational surveillance.

Measurement without meaning is not just ineffective; it can be harmful.

Telling the Right Story

Ultimately, measurement is not just about numbers. It's about the story we tell about progress.

That story should include:

- Insight breakthroughs
- Identity exploration
- Emotional shifts
- Relationship transformation
- Systemic navigation

The best dashboards don't just show outcomes; they reveal meaning.

The storytelling function of measurement infrastructure serves as the translation layer between quantitative data and qualitative transformation. Like architects who create visual representations that help clients understand how abstract blueprints will become living spaces, coaches must help organizations understand how measurement data connects to real human development.

Such translation activity comes to the fore when communicating with stakeholders who will be less familiar with the sophisticated metrics of emotional and cultural growth than with hard business measures. Value needs to be shown through the medium by which organizational leaders communicate but with such richness and nuance as to maintain the transformational impact of the story.

Successful narration on the impact of coaching typically needs several narrative strands: the personal change story, the team growth story, the organizational culture story, and the systemic change story. Machine tools will assist with identifying trends across these varying levels, but human intuition is needed to thread these together into cohesive narratives that will maintain investment in the use of coaching infrastructure.

What ICI Tracks

At ICI, we blend:

- Quantitative metrics: Session frequency, self-assessments, goal completion
- Qualitative reflections: Written insights, coach observations, identity impact
- Client-defined success: "What will tell you this coaching was worth it?"

At ICI, measurement has nothing to do with productivity scores. Coaching is a mirror that reflects reality, a map that guides progress, and a catalyst that sparks transformation.

As we measure coaching's impact in the AI era, we must be careful not to lose the essence of the work in the speed of the system. The ICI methodology for measurement mirrors the same principles of infrastructure that guide our approach to coaching itself.

We design systems for measurement that can be scaled while preserving the human relationships that drive transformation. We create systems for visibility that strengthen coaching effectiveness without replacing the judgment of the coach. We build tracking mechanisms that serve the development needs of the client rather than the monitoring needs of the organization.

This balance requires constant calibration. As AI tools grow more sophisticated, the temptation increases to lean on algorithmic assessments rather than human wisdom. Our measurement infrastructure must always include safeguards that prevent this drift toward automation, ensuring that technology serves human development rather than substituting for it.

Illustrative Example

To see how intent shapes outcomes, consider two ways of evaluating the same coaching program:

Scenario 1: AI-Only Approach

A platform tracks every interaction, analyzes sentiment, and produces performance reports for managers.

Results: Participants feel observed rather than supported. Coaches focus on short-term metrics, and authentic growth remains invisible.

Scenario 2: AI + Culturally Responsive Coaching

Here, AI tools surface patterns for coaches and clients, who co-define success measures. Insights remain confidential unless clients choose to share them. Aggregate data informs systemic learning without surveillance.

Results: Participants report higher trust, greater willingness to explore vulnerable areas, and more sustainable growth. Coaches gain richer insight into cultural context, and organizations see systemic barriers without compromising individual safety.

The difference is not in the tools themselves but in intent: whether measurement infrastructure serves organizational control or human development.

Chapter 8 Practice Lab

Activity 1: Philosophical Evaluation for Measurement

- Foundation check: List five indicators you currently use to measure whether coaching is working. Note if each indicator measures external behavior or inner change.
- Co-measurement design: Write five questions you would ask a client to help them set their own success indicators. Design a process for revisiting these indicators over time.
- Cultural responsiveness review: Review a measurement system you've used. Identify three ways it could misinterpret growth for someone from a different cultural background. Redesign one part of the system to make it more inclusive.

Activity 2: Story Translation Workshop

- Personal story: Write a short account of a coaching transformation that highlights inner change.
- Manager's view: Reframe the same story for a supervisor who values outcomes.
- Cultural lens: Add a version that highlights cultural or identity dimensions.
- Systemic impact: Connect three individual stories into a memo showing organizational culture trends. Create a simple graphic that shows ROI without reducing people to numbers.

- Co-measurement session: Draft a quarterly reflection template where clients define their own progress, linking it to values and long-term goals.

Activity 3: AI Tool Evaluation

- Tool analysis: Research three AI tools marketed for measuring coaching. For each, list what data it collects, how it analyzes it, and the outputs provided.
- Ethical safeguards: Design safeguards that let you use these tools without breaching trust. Write a consent process that gives clients a choice in what gets measured.
- Alternative metrics: Identify three coaching outcomes that resist quantification. Propose ways to track these through client self-reflection rather than external monitoring.

Reflection Questions

Measurement Philosophy:

- What assumptions regarding human growth are built into the assessment systems that you use or see?
- How do you distinguish between measuring coaching compliance versus coaching transformation?
- When data and your coaching intuition conflict, which do you trust more, and why?

Cultural dimensions:

- How might your own cultural background influence which indicators you see as evidence of growth?
- What leadership development trends in your practice might be overlooked by standard measurement systems?

- How can measurement be redesigned to reflect different cultural approaches to feedback, goals, and relationships?

Ethical boundaries:

- Where should the line be drawn between measuring coaching effectiveness and surveilling coaching participants?
- How do you balance organizational accountability needs with client privacy and autonomy?
- What role do coaches play in preventing measurement systems from reinforcing inequities?

AI integration:

- How can AI tools enhance measurement without replacing human judgment about what constitutes meaningful transformation?
- What protections would help ensure that insights generated by AI support coaching relationships instead of organizational monitoring?
- How frequently must the systems measuring AI for bias and cultural sensitivity be audited?

Future preparation:

- As the ability to measure AI becomes increasingly advanced, how will you ensure that you prioritize the metrics that truly matter for human development?
- What new competencies might coaches need for interpreting and contextualizing AI-generated measurement data?
- How can measurement systems evolve to capture transformation that hasn't been previously recognized or valued?

Looking Ahead

This chapter has explored the complex terrain of measuring coaching effectiveness in an AI-augmented world.

Sarah's story illustrates the fundamental challenge: the most meaningful transformations resist traditional measurement, yet organizations still need evidence of return.

The infrastructure metaphor helps us frame this challenge as a design problem: like cities balancing traffic efficiency with community life, coaching programs must balance accountability with depth.

The solution is not to choose between metrics and meaning, but to create systems that hold both. Co-measurement ensures clients define their own success. Culturally responsive practices protect against bias. AI enhances visibility but only when guided by human interpretation.

The systems we design today will determine how the profession of coaching evolves tomorrow.

In Chapter 6, we examined how coaches maintain presence and cultural responsiveness when AI enters the coaching room. This chapter widened the lens to the organizational level: how systems measure outcomes at scale without losing humanity. Both are essential. Presence safeguards authenticity in the room, and ethical measurement ensures that authenticity is not lost in translation when results are shared with the wider system.

As we turn to the next chapter, we look ahead: what competencies will future coaches need, and how must coach training itself evolve for a world where AI augmentation is no longer experimental but expected?

PART IV
PREPARING FOR THE FUTURE

Infrastructure for an uncertain future needs a different type of engineering. Regular construction projects proceed based on detailed drawings toward known specs. But when you're assembling human infrastructure for the age of artificial intelligence, you're designing systems that will need to accommodate evolutions you're not yet certain you'll encounter.

Planners encounter the same challenges when they plan for future residents of cities who will change and grow over generations. They will not exactly know what technologies will develop, how working patterns will change, or what new challenges the residents will encounter. So they develop flexible infrastructures that will accommodate greater capacity, accommodate new uses, and fit with yet-unimagined technologies.

The same holds true with the future of coaching in the age of AI. We're not simply training coaches for the current tools; we're cultivating skills that will continue to pay off as the technology advances. We're creating human infrastructure that will not diminish but gain momentum as the pace of technology keeps speeding up.

Part IV addresses the challenge of preparing for what doesn't exist yet while staying grounded in timeless principles of human development. The four chapters in this section examine different aspects of future readiness, from individual coach development to organizational capacity building to the broader evolution of the coaching profession.

- *Chapter 9: The Future of Coach Training* examines how coach education must evolve to prepare practitioners for AI-augmented practice. We explore the shift from mastering fixed methodologies to developing adaptive capacities: emotional intelligence, cultural fluency, ethical reasoning, and technological wisdom. You'll discover why future coaches need what we call empathic adaptability, the ability to flex across contexts while maintaining human depth. This chapter includes practical frameworks for updating coach training curricula and assessment methods that honor both technological competence and relational skill.

- *Chapter 10: Preparing for What Doesn't Exist (Yet)* tackles the problem of designing resilient coaching infrastructure where the environment continues to change. We discuss how to cultivate future fluency: the ability to foresee change, manage ambiguity, and implement change with integrity. This chapter considers future trends that will redefine the practice of coaching, ranging from the application of virtual reality to integrating global culture into the next generation of human–AI co-creation. You'll discover how to remain one step ahead of change with an eye toward maintaining what is deeply human in coaching.

- *Chapter 11: Coaching Futures—The Skills Tomorrow Demands* synthesizes insights from across the book into a comprehensive framework for next-generation coaching competencies. We examine five core capabilities that will distinguish exceptional coaches in the AI era: systems thinking, cultural intelligence, technological discernment, adaptive presence, and ethical leadership. This chapter provides diagnostic tools for assessing current capabilities and development plans for strengthening future readiness.

- *Chapter 12: Where AI Meets Empathy™* brings together all threads into a vision for coaching's role in creating more humane technological integration. We explore how coaches can serve as bridges between human wisdom and artificial capability, helping individuals and organizations navigate change without losing their essential humanity. This final chapter includes a call to action for the coaching profession and practical steps for implementing the frameworks throughout your practice.

As a whole, these chapters struggle with fundamental questions regarding the future of human development during an age of artificial intelligence. What will coaches need to be capable of when technology continues to gain speed? How will coaching education prepare practitioners for issues yet to be imagined? How will coaches also help decide how artificial intelligence is incorporated into human systems?

The analogy with physical infrastructure also predominates for all of Part IV. Just as urban areas require long-term thinking that weighs current needs against future flexibility, the coach infrastructure must weigh near-term effectiveness against long-term flexibility. We're not merely instructing coaches in the use of present tools for artificial intelligence; we're developing the human capability that is always vital, regardless of how technology evolves.

This work requires what urban planners call adaptive capacity, the ability to modify systems based on changing conditions without compromising their fundamental purpose. For coaches, this translates into empathic adaptability, the ability to maintain relational depth while integrating new technologies, to preserve cultural responsiveness while scaling globally, and to uphold ethical standards while embracing innovation.

The next few chapters delve into how to cultivate this adaptive capability on all the following levels: individual practitioner development, organizational coaching programs, education systems for the professions, and the broader profession itself. We examine the opportunities for doing the most good and the least bad during the pace of fast-changing technology.

Throughout Part IV, we put the human beings who are the ultimate object of all integration of technology at the center. Artificial intelligence isn't progressing for its own purposes; it's progressing due to the fact that human beings are programming it for the accomplishment of human ends. Coaches hold the key to ensuring the ends are human flourishing instead of optimization.

The future that we are preparing for is not pre-written. Rather, it will be shaped by the choices that we make today on how to integrate artificial intelligence with human development processes. Coaches have the honor, and responsibility, to help shape these choices so that technological capability will enhance human wisdom rather than replace it.

The systems we develop today will shape the generations ahead to see AI as an instrument for freedom or restriction, connection or disconnection, equity or marginalization. Our decisions regarding coach education, moral compasses, cultural competence, and human-centered design will cascade through the decades ahead in the practice of coaching.

It's all about hope in the long run, hope born not of wishful thinking but of preparation. We cannot foresee exactly how the future will turn out but can cultivate the human potential required to face it with wisdom, courage, and compassion. We can create a culture of coaching that becomes stronger rather than weaker when stressed, that becomes larger rather than smaller when scaled, that supports human flourishing no matter what new technologies develop.

The foundations are set. The structures are proven. We look to the future horizon, readying the field of coaching for whatever lies ahead with the timeless foundation of facilitating individual human change, relationship by relationship.

The Future of Coach Training

Emily Carter, a European–American coach educator, had spent eight years training coaches when the panic set in. As the dean of a university-affiliated coach training program, she was responsible for preparing future practitioners to meet International Coaching Federation (ICF) standards while also keeping pace with the changing realities of leadership development. Her programs had earned a reputation for rigor and reliability.

But scanning through the latest reports on AI integration from her office, she was struck with the enormity of change on the horizon.

"How do I prepare coaches for tools that don't even exist yet?" she asked her colleague and longtime friend, Dr. Michael Park, over their monthly coffee meeting. "My current curriculum covers everything from active listening to goal setting. But now I need to add AI ethics, cultural responsiveness, digital presence, and technology discernment? Where do I even begin?"

Michael, who had recently completed advanced training in integrating AI tools into coaching practice, set his cup down thoughtfully. "What if you're thinking about this the wrong way?" he replied.

Emily frowned. "What do you mean?"

"You're thinking about adding more content to the same old framework. But what if the framework itself needs to change? What if instead of teaching fixed models, you focused on cultivating adaptive mindsets?"

Emily leaned back, unconvinced. "Go on."

"Your students already know the GROW model. They can give 360 feedback and set goals. Those are valuable skills, but they're also the skills that AI will eventually replicate or augment. What AI can never replicate is cultural intuition, ethical reasoning, or the ability to hold space for identity-based transformation."

In the weeks that followed, Emily began redesigning her program. She shifted from teaching a long list of models toward cultivating what she came to call empathic adaptability: the underlying capacities that allow coaches to remain effective no matter what new technologies or cultural contexts they encounter.

Instead of dedicating three weeks to memorizing methodologies, she spent one week on models and two weeks on practicing how to adapt any model to varied cultural conditions. Instead of rehearsing standardized questioning techniques, students practiced discernment: recognizing when to ask, when to pause, and when silence itself was the most powerful tool. Instead of simply learning assessment instruments, they developed the ability to help clients co-create their own measures of meaningful progress.

Six months later, when Emily's trainees encountered their first AI-enabled coaching platform, they approached it with curiosity rather than dread. One reflected: "I wasn't wondering if the AI was right or wrong. I wanted to know how its insights could help my client grow in their cultural context. The technology became an accompaniment, not a replacement."

Emily realized she had moved from training coaches how to manage established systems to preparing coaches who could build better systems on the fly.

* * *

Emily's story reflects a fundamental shift in how human infrastructure must be developed for the age of artificial intelligence. Traditional training assumes stable roles and predictable skill needs. But in a rapidly changing technological environment, coaches need adaptive capacity, flexibility that holds under pressure, rather than fixed competencies.

Like architects who design seismically safe buildings with flexible foundations, coach education must prioritize the underlying abilities that remain relevant no matter how technology evolves. Resilience in this era comes not from resisting change but from cultivating empathic adaptability: the capacity to bend without breaking, to integrate new tools while staying rooted in human connection.

From Frameworks to Fluidity

Traditional coach training emphasizes structure:

- GROW model
- ICF core competencies
- Credentialing benchmarks

These are important. But in an AI-augmented world, they are only the foundation.

Coaches must shift from rigid technique to adaptive presence:

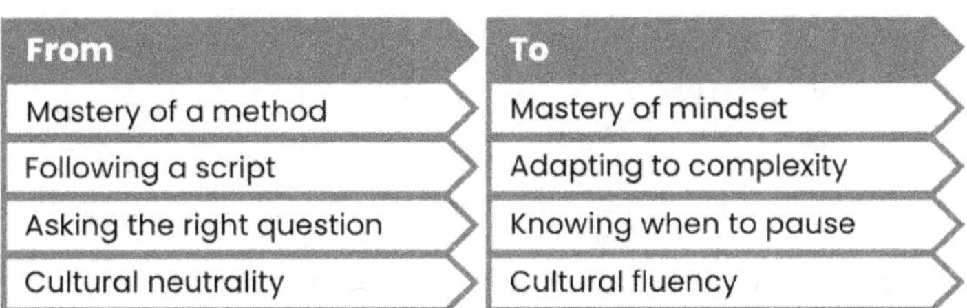

From	To
Mastery of a method	Mastery of mindset
Following a script	Adapting to complexity
Asking the right question	Knowing when to pause
Cultural neutrality	Cultural fluency

This shift requires prioritizing fluidity over formula. And it calls for training that cultivates presence, self-reflection, and ethical discernment, not just performance.

The infrastructure metaphor shows why this shift matters. Rigid systems hold under stable conditions but fracture under stress. Flexible systems, like bridges with expansion joints or buildings designed for earthquakes, bend without breaking. In the same way, coaches trained only in one methodology may falter when new technologies emerge, while those trained in adaptable mindsets can thrive across contexts.

What coach training must develop is a kind of modular design: capacities that hold steady even as tools, cultures, and environments change. Like a city grid that can accommodate new transit or energy systems, adaptive coaches can integrate new technologies without losing their core human foundation.

What Coaches Need to Learn Now

1. AI Awareness

Understand how generative AI works, not as engineers but as ethical practitioners. Coaches should know what data trains AI, how bias is encoded, when to challenge outputs, and how to use AI as a co-creator rather than a crutch.

2. Cultural Responsiveness

Treat social identity, systemic inequity, and cross-cultural communication as essentials, not electives.

3. Coaching the Whole Person

Hold space for the human behind performance: identity, emotions, resistance, and vision.

4. Digital Presence

Cultivate relational depth across screens, platforms, languages, and time zones. Presence must translate digitally.

These competencies are the load-bearing elements of coaching infrastructure in the AI age. Like the steel beams that support modern buildings, they must be strong enough to hold whatever technological changes are built on top of them.

But beams alone don't make a building. Integration matters. AI awareness without cultural responsiveness can perpetuate bias. Digital presence without emotional depth risks hollow connection. Coaching the whole person without systems awareness overlooks the larger forces shaping growth.

Effective coach training must therefore weave these elements into an integrated foundation that endures across contexts and technologies. This is what distinguishes coaching infrastructure from a loose collection of skills.

Illustrative Example:
Readiness Before the First Session

In a leadership development initiative, a healthcare organization onboarded 60 mid-level managers into coaching. Many of them had never experienced coaching before. Unfamiliar with the process, several participants expressed anxiety, confusion, or skepticism.

To support readiness, the organization piloted a lightweight AI-powered intake assistant: a tool designed to answer questions about confidentiality, coaching goals, and expectations. In addition to standard intake forms, the assistant offered reflective prompts and created a short narrative summary for the coach.

One participant remarked: "I thought it was just going to be paperwork, but it felt like someone already understood what I needed."

Architectural View:

- Clear foundations – Trust and cultural awareness created space for coaches to voice ethical concerns.
- Proper scaffolding – AI tools and analysis frameworks supported bias detection without requiring technical expertise.
- Structural integrity – Ethical frameworks reinforced professional boundaries and client wellbeing.
- Successful completion – Coaches gained confidence to raise ethical concerns and guide organizational leaders toward responsible AI implementation.

Link to model: This illustration highlights Phase 4 of ICI's 5-phase integration model, coach training + AI ethics modules, which equips coaches to practice ethical reasoning in AI-integrated environments.

Illustrative Example:
Phase 4 – Ethics as a Coaching Competency

Case Title: *Coaching with a Conscience*

Challenge:
Coaches working in a tech firm that was integrating AI into HR systems expressed concern about operating without clear ethical guidance. Solution: In this illustration, a coach training + AI ethics module equips coaches to question systems, recognize bias, and support ethical reflection when organizations adopt AI-enabled processes.

Outcome:
Coaches shifted from passive observers to active ethical guides. "Now I see it as part of my stance, not just my skillset."

Architectural View:

- Clear foundations – Cultural understanding and trust acknowledged coaches' legitimate concerns about working in ethically ambiguous situations. The training emphasized both conceptual grounding and practical application of ethical reasoning in real coaching scenarios.

- Proper scaffolding – AI tools and support systems helped coaches recognize bias patterns and ask systems-level questions without requiring technical expertise. The module provided ethical analysis frameworks that could be applied across different technological contexts.

- Structural integrity – Ethical frameworks reinforced professional boundaries and the responsibility to advocate for client wellbeing, even when organizational pressures prioritized efficiency.

- Successful completion – Coaches developed confidence to raise ethical concerns and guide organizational leaders toward more responsible AI implementation. The infrastructure supported coaches in becoming ethical leaders rather than passive service providers.

Link to Model: This illustration highlights Phase 4 of ICI's 5-phase integration model, coach training + AI ethics modules, which prepares coaches to navigate AI-integrated environments with clarity and confidence.

ICI's Approach

At the Institute for Coaching Innovation (ICI), we believe coach training must do more than meet today's standards; it must prepare practitioners for tomorrow's uncertainties. Our approach is built on three principles: innovation, equity, and impact.

- Culturally grounded – We treat cultural awareness and identity as structural foundations, not electives. Listening for identity is a core competency in every coaching interaction.

- AI-integrated – We weave technology into training as scaffolding, not as replacement. From reflective journaling prompts to feedback augmentation, we teach coaches how to use AI ethically and responsibly.

- Modular and global – Like modular construction that adapts to varied terrains, our curriculum is designed for diverse learners across industries, geographies, and delivery formats.

- Credential-aligned – Our programs meet established standards while building the adaptive capacities—empathy, ethical reasoning, cultural fluency—that tomorrow's coaches will require.

This integrated approach reflects our conviction that coach education must move beyond skill collection to infrastructure building. We are not only training coaches to practice today; we are cultivating a profession resilient enough to thrive in an AI-augmented world.

The New Credential: Empathic Adaptability

In the future, coaching credentials may still require logged hours, supervision, and demonstrated competency. But the most valued coaches will be recognized not only for technical compliance; they will be known for empathic adaptability.

Empathic adaptability is the ability to flex across contexts, integrate new tools, and always center the human. It is not another method to memorize, but a capacity to sustain presence, ethics, and cultural responsiveness in any environment.

The qualities of empathic adaptability include:

- Cultural humility – Recognizing that identity and context shape every coaching conversation
- Technological adaptability – Learning to work with AI and other tools as supports, not substitutes
- Emotional presence – Holding space for the whole person, especially when clients are navigating technological or systemic change
- Strategic thinking – Guiding not only individuals but also organizations through ethical and cultural complexity

This idea is not entirely new. Wisdom traditions have long understood that empathy enables adaptation without erasing identity. For example, the *Schitsu'umsh* (Coeur d'Alene Tribe) principle of *snukwnkhwtskhwts'mi'ls ɫ stsee'nidmsh* teaches that empathetic understanding allows people to adapt while staying rooted in core values (Coeur d'Alene Tribe and University of Idaho, 2015).

Empathic adaptability brings that same principle into coach education. It provides the structural integrity the profession needs to thrive in an AI-augmented world.

Coach training, therefore, is no longer about keeping pace with standards. It is about preparing for what does not yet exist, building a profession that can bend without breaking, adapt without losing its human depth, and lead technological change rather than react to it.

Illustrative Example

To illustrate how different training approaches prepare coaches for AI-augmented practice, consider how two coach development programs might address the same technological challenge.

Scenario 1: AI-Only Approach

Approach: The coach development program emphasizes technological competency above all else. Participants spend extensive time learning to use various AI coaching tools, understanding algorithmic outputs, and optimizing their use of automated systems. The curriculum focuses on efficiency gains, productivity improvements, and technical troubleshooting. Success is measured through proficiency tests and AI-driven client satisfaction scores.

Results: Coaches emerge technically proficient but limited. They struggle when AI tools produce culturally insensitive recommendations or when clients face challenges beyond algorithmic solutions. Many report feeling more like AI operators than human development professionals. When systems fail, these coaches lack the underlying human skills needed to sustain effective practice.

Scenario 2: AI + Culturally Responsive Coaching

Approach: Another program integrates empathic adaptability alongside technological literacy. Participants learn to use AI tools but also spend equal time cultivating cultural responsiveness, ethical reasoning, and emotional presence. Technology is taught not as an isolated skill set but as part of a human-centered coaching philosophy.

Results: Coaches graduate confident about using AI creatively, while sustaining strong client relationships. They can challenge algorithmic bias, adapt across cultures, and integrate technological insights with personal wisdom. When tools evolve or malfunction, they remain effective because their foundation is human rather than technological.

Architectural View:

The contrast shows two different infrastructure strategies. Training that builds only on technical scaffolding collapses when stress tested.

Training that invests in flexible foundations—empathy, cultural fluency, and ethical reasoning—creates resilient structures that can bend without breaking as technology changes.

Chapter 9 Practice Lab

Activity 1: Adaptive Capacity Assessment

- Foundations: List five coaching skills you rely on most. Note how each skill would need to adapt in an AI-augmented environment.

- Scaffolding: Choose one recent coaching challenge. Reflect on how cultural humility, flexibility with technology, emotional presence, and strategic thinking shaped your response.

- Structural integrity: Identify your strongest and weakest dimensions of empathic adaptability. Create a plan to strengthen the weaker ones while reinforcing your strengths.

- Future readiness: Research three emerging AI tools. For each, write one guideline that would keep its use human centered.

Activity 2: Ethical Reasoning Development

- Review a sample AI-generated coaching observation. Identify possible cultural or demographic biases. Reframe it through a culturally responsive lens.

- Draft a short personal ethics statement for AI in coaching. Include boundaries around privacy, cultural respect, and client choice.

- Map the systemic ripple effects: How might AI adoption affect power, equity, and development in your organization? Write two ways a coach could advocate for responsible use.

Activity 3: Cultural Fluency Integration

- Map three cultural contexts where you may offer coaching. Note values around hierarchy, communication, and feedback.

- Practice an identity-affirming coaching question that treats cultural differences as an asset.

- Assess your global readiness: What tools support cross-cultural coaching across languages and time zones? How will you maintain presence and connection in digital settings?

Reflection Questions

Personal development:

- What coaching talents come most naturally to you, and how could they transfer to an AI-augmented environment?

- How does your attitude toward new technology, whether excitement, skepticism, or caution, affect your flexibility?

- How has your cultural heritage shaped your assumptions about effective coaching, and what blind spots might exist?

Professional development:

- As routine activities become increasingly automated, which human skills would you like to strengthen?

- How do you balance established methods with adapting to client needs, and how might this process shift with AI integration?

- What ethical challenges have you faced, and how would you address similar situations when tools are AI-based?

Future preparation:

- What emerging trends may influence your coaching approach?

- How do you stay current professionally, and what additional learning could help you adapt to technological changes?
- How would you like to influence AI application in coaching rather than passively follow it?

Cultural and systemic responsiveness:

- How do you observe and respond to cultural context in coaching relationships?
- Which assumptions about "universal" coaching principles may actually reflect cultural bias?
- What responsibility do coaches have for ensuring AI is used ethically and equitably within organizations?

Moving Forward

This chapter has explored how coach training must evolve to meet the technological and cultural complexities of the AI era. Emily's story illustrates the shift from teaching fixed methods to cultivating adaptive capacities that remain valuable no matter how tools or platforms change.

The infrastructure metaphor reminds us that training designed only for stable environments will fail when conditions shift abruptly. Just as architects design buildings with flexible foundations for seismic safety, coach education must develop empathic adaptability, ethical reasoning, and cultural fluency as the structural integrity of the profession.

The practices we outlined, from AI awareness to cultural responsiveness, coaching the whole person, and cultivating digital presence, demonstrate that coach training is no longer about collecting competencies. It is about weaving them into an integrated foundation strong enough to support future challenges.

Coach education that embraces this approach prepares practitioners to be ethical leaders, cultural translators, and adaptive builders of human infrastructure. It ensures that technology enhances rather than diminishes the human heart of coaching.

As we turn to the next chapter, we look outward: how to prepare for what doesn't exist yet. If coach training equips individuals with adaptive capacity, Chapter 10 examines how organizations, and the profession as a whole, can design systems resilient enough to thrive in an uncertain future.

Preparing for What Doesn't Exist (Yet)

Marcus Thompson had spent twelve years leading talent development at an international manufacturing company when the questions began, the ones that kept him awake at night. Normally steady and forward-looking, he prided himself on preparing his people for what was coming next. But the speed of artificial intelligence unsettled even him.

"I've been training managers the same way for more than a decade," he confessed to his longtime mentor Dr. Patricia Williams, during one of their quarterly calls. "Active listening. Feedback delivery. Performance management. Conflict resolution. But what happens when AI runs sentiment analysis better than humans? What happens when virtual reality can simulate any scenario for practice? What skills will my managers really need in five years?"

Patricia, who had spent thirty years in leadership development before moving into coaching, let the question sit. "Tell me what's keeping you up at night, Marcus."

He sighed. "I'm preparing people for jobs that may not exist in the form I imagine. Traditional leadership skills are still important, but they're not enough. I don't know how to teach for a future I can't predict."

Patricia leaned in. "What if the problem isn't about prediction at all? Instead of asking which skills will be needed, what if you focused on the mindsets that let leaders adapt to whatever shows up?"

Marcus frowned. "I'm not sure I follow."

"Think about the leaders in your company who thrive during change. They don't always guess right about what's coming, but they stay curious. They build relationships that can weather disruption. They use judgment that holds even when the rules change."

Her words landed. Over the following months, Marcus began rethinking his entire program. Instead of preparing managers for specific situations, he started cultivating what he called adaptive leadership infrastructure: the capacity to build trust quickly, stay grounded under pressure, and maintain human connection in increasingly digital environments.

Six months later, when his company launched an AI-driven performance system, his leaders didn't panic. They approached the tool with curiosity, used it to enhance, not replace, their judgment, and guided their teams through the transition without losing trust.

One manager told Marcus, "I didn't know exactly what was coming, but I felt prepared for whatever it was. The AI gave us data, but I had the relationships and judgment to know what that data meant for my people."

Marcus realized he had shifted from training leaders to respond to specific scenarios to preparing leaders who could succeed in any scenario they faced.

* * *

Marcus's experience illustrates the central challenge of preparing for the future: when conditions shift faster than anyone can predict, training people for specific scenarios isn't enough. The real task is to build adaptive capacity, the ability to flex, respond, and stay grounded no matter what emerges.

The infrastructure metaphor makes this clear. Cities designed only for today's traffic quickly choke when new technologies arrive. But cities built with flexible routes, modular systems, and expansion space can absorb change with minimal disruption.

Leadership development and coaching face the same problem. Programs that prepare people only for today's demands become obsolete as soon as new tools appear. But programs that focus on adaptive infrastructure, skills like emotional intelligence, cultural fluency, ethical reasoning, and systems thinking, retain their value across any technological environment.

So the question is not, "Which skills do we teach now?"

The question is: "How do we prepare leaders and coaches to thrive when the future keeps changing?"

The Future Is Not a Template

For years, coach training followed a predictable path:

- Learn a model
- Log hours
- Demonstrate competencies
- Earn a credential

Today, the future calls for something different. Coaches must be:

- Technologically literate without being defined by tools
- Emotionally intelligent in the face of pressure
- Culturally responsive across diverse contexts
- Systemically aware of forces beyond the individual
- Future-ready, while grounded in the present

At ICI, we prepare coaches not only to navigate the present but to shape what comes next.

Engineers call it antifragile design: systems that grow stronger under stress. Traditional coach education has aimed for resilience; the future requires coaches who thrive in uncertainty and help others do the same. That means moving beyond applying existing frameworks to creating new ones when conditions demand it; beyond rule lists to ethical judgment when there is no precedent; beyond cultural "tips" to cultural intelligence that bridges differences that don't fit tidy categories.

Predictable problems yield to specific training.

Unpredictable problems require foundational abilities that apply regardless of circumstances.

Illustrative Example: Phase 4: Ethics as a Coaching Competency

Challenge:

A cohort of experienced coaches was asked to support a national tech firm integrating AI into HR. Many felt uneasy, concerned about bias, privacy, and unclear guardrails. Some admitted they didn't know how to ask the right questions.

Approach:

An AI + ethics module equipped them to:

- Recognize algorithmic bias without technical expertise
- Ask systems-level questions
- Hold ethical reflection amid speed and surveillance pressures

Outcome:

Coaches shifted from passive observers to ethical guides. One reflected: "I didn't realize I was allowed to question the system. Now it's part of my stance."

Architectural View:

- Foundations: Trust and cultural awareness legitimized ethical concern.
- Scaffolding: Tools and frameworks supported bias detection and systems inquiry.
- Structural integrity: Professional boundaries prioritized wellbeing over efficiency.
- Completion: Coaches gained confidence to guide responsible AI use.

Link to Model: Phase 4—*coach training + ai ethics modules* strengthen adaptive capacity for unknown dilemmas.

Three Mindsets for the Future-Ready Coach

Curiosity Over Certainty

AI tools will evolve. So will client needs. The best coaches lead with curiosity, not expertise. They ask better questions, not faster ones.

Curiosity rather than certainty generates learning infrastructure that is flexible instead of defensive. Coaches who enter the unknown with curiosity, rather than the pressure to seem expert, model for clients how to face uncertainty with confidence. This proves especially useful when working with AI, which often produces surprising insights or unexpected advice.

Integrity in Innovation

Just because a technology can do something doesn't mean it should. Coaches must serve as the ethical compass in organizations adopting AI, prioritizing equity, privacy, and humanity.

Integrity in innovation provides ethical architecture strong enough to evaluate new tools by human values rather than efficiency alone. As AI capabilities grow exponentially, coaches need standards that distinguish innovation that enhances human flourishing from innovation that serves only organizational convenience.

Presence Over Performance

In a world of relentless optimization, presence is radical. Coaches who slow down, listen deeply, and stay connected become invaluable leadership partners.

Presence over performance builds relational architecture that sustains human connection even when technology increases speed and scale. By choosing presence over output, coaches provide an organizational differentiator that supports individual growth and systemic wellness alike.

Ethical Coaching in an AI World

As AI becomes more integrated into leadership, education, and health, coaches will face increasingly complex questions:

- When is AI-enhanced insight helpful, and when is it intrusive?
- How do we coach clients through algorithmic bias or surveillance anxiety?
- What does agency look like in systems where decisions are machine-shaped?

These are not technical questions. They are human questions, and they represent the future of coaching.

The enabling infrastructure for addressing them is not technical expertise but moral imagination: the ability to see how present choices shape human flourishing tomorrow. Coaches need thought tools to explore questions with no clear answers, to make judgments where risks are undefined, and to preserve human values when technology pressures organizations to optimize rather than empathize.

Building this ethical infrastructure requires practice with moral complexity, exposure to diverse value systems, and experience holding multiple perspectives at once. It calls for coaches who can help clients balance individual growth with systemic responsibility, and technological capability with human limitation.

Consider a simple example: a coach supporting a leader whose company is adopting an AI-driven hiring system. The system increases speed but also introduces bias in screening applicants. Ethical coaching here is less about teaching compliance than about asking deeper questions: What values should guide hiring? Whose definitions of "fit" are embedded in the algorithm? What responsibility does the leader have to challenge efficiency when it undermines equity?

Such challenges escalate when coaching crosses borders. Ethical lenses shift. One culture may prioritize the individual, another the collective; one may value relationships over speed, another innovation over tradition. Coaches need ethical foundations strong enough to carry unseen loads, like bridges designed with safety margins beyond today's traffic, so they can honor cultural distinctions while still upholding universal values of dignity and humanity.

A Global Reality: Coaching Across Borders

The 2023 ICF Global Coaching Study found that 83% of coaches work across national or cultural boundaries. Coaching is now an international profession, which means empathy must expand beyond Western defaults and be reshaped by cultural context.

In Japan, high-context communication norms require coaches to listen for what is unsaid. In Latin America, relational trust often comes before goal setting. In both cases, emotional intelligence remains constant, but its expression shifts across cultures.

As coaching spreads worldwide, the challenge resembles global construction: what works in one terrain may collapse in another, not because of poor design but because it was built on different cultural premises. Effective coaching infrastructure requires working with deeper assumptions: individual vs. collective priorities, linear vs. cyclical time, direct vs. indirect conflict, hierarchical vs. egalitarian power.

This challenge becomes sharper when using AI tools trained largely on Western data. Coaches must be able to recognize when algorithmic suggestions are reproducing cultural bias rather than offering universal wisdom and know how to adapt practice accordingly.

The future of coaching lies not in a single universal method, but in adaptive capacity: frameworks that are globally consistent and locally responsive. Like engineers designing structures that can flex across varied climates and terrains, coach education must prepare practitioners who can honor local culture while maintaining professional effectiveness.

If we succeed, coaching will not only travel across borders; it will build bridges of understanding where borders once divided. This is the human infrastructure our profession can offer, practices resilient enough to meet global challenges and humane enough to preserve what makes each culture distinct.

Coaching Is a Future Technology

Paradoxically, coaching itself may be the most future-proof technology we have. It:

- Strengthens emotional resilience

- Encourages identity exploration
- Cultivates self-leadership
- Develops adaptive learning
- Creates space for values, meaning, and purpose

AI can support all of this, but it cannot replace it. Algorithms may simulate empathy, but only humans can hold silence with a client, notice a subtle shift in tone, or help someone reconnect with their own values.

Think of coaching as living infrastructure. It flexes, grows, and adapts to whatever new tools or systems emerge. Where machines provide speed, coaching provides depth. Where AI maps patterns, coaching restores perspective. Where technology optimizes performance, coaching reclaims presence and purpose.

We are not training coaches merely to survive disruption.

We are training them to guide humanity through it, with wisdom, courage, and empathy.

That is the mission of the Institute for Coaching Innovation.

That is the heart of Where AI Meets Empathy™.

That is the future we are building together.

Illustrative Example

Challenge:

Coach training programs worldwide face a common dilemma: should they emphasize technical proficiency with AI tools, or focus on building adaptive human capacities that endure as technology evolves?

Scenario 1: AI-Only Approach

Approach:

A program centers on tool fluency, teaching coaches to master the latest platforms, optimize efficiency, and troubleshoot technical issues. Success is measured by adoption rates, productivity metrics, and AI-generated satisfaction scores.

Results:

Coaches graduate as proficient operators but unprepared for surprise challenges. When confronted with biased algorithms, cultural misunderstandings, or privacy dilemmas, they lack the ethical and cultural judgment to respond.

Scenario 2: AI + Culturally Responsive Coaching

Approach:

Another program integrates empathic adaptability with tool literacy. Coaches still learn AI basics, but equal focus is placed on ethical reasoning, cultural intelligence, systems thinking, and emotional presence. Success is measured by transformation outcomes, cultural responsiveness demonstrations, and the ability to sustain human connection across contexts.

Results:

These coaches meet uncertainty with curiosity and discernment. They evaluate new tools through ethical and cultural filters, adapt practices to local contexts, and preserve human connection regardless of technology shifts.

Architectural View:

Tech-only training is like unsupported scaffolding. It looks stable but collapses when stress tested.

Adaptive training builds flexible foundations, structures that bend without breaking as conditions change.

Chapter 10 Practice Lab

Activity 1: Future Scenario Planning

- Identify 3 trends (e.g., VR training, brain–computer interfaces, climate migration). For each, name one opportunity and one risk.
- Select one ambiguous scenario. Ask: which foundational abilities (EI, cultural fluency, ethics, systems thinking) will matter most? Draft a plan to strengthen them now.
- Practice holding multiple futures. Write a decision rubric for when information is incomplete.

Activity 2: Ethical Infrastructure Building

- Recall 3 ethical dilemmas. What values were in conflict? How would AI or cultural differences have altered the stakes?
- Map stakeholders in one organization. Where might client needs and organizational goals clash? Draft two approaches that honor both.
- Study 3 ethical traditions (e.g., Ubuntu, Confucian ethics, Indigenous reciprocity). Apply each lens to the same coaching challenge. Note how your reasoning shifts.

Activity 3: Adaptive Presence Development

- Coach across three mediums (video, audio-only, written/async). Note what supports connection; adjust accordingly.

- Partner with someone from a different culture. Observe silence, directness, and hierarchy norms. Adjust without losing authenticity.

- Rehearse calm presence in high-stress simulations. Develop three "reset" strategies to ground yourself and contain client anxiety.

Reflection Questions

Future Preparedness Assessment

- Do you feel more nervous or excited thinking about the future of your profession? What does this reveal about how you handle uncertainty?

- Which human coaching capacities will matter no matter how technology evolves?

- How do you currently access information on new advances in your area? What adjustments could enable you to remain information, fully adaptable without becoming overwrought?

Ethical Foundation

- Which moral principles guide your practice? How might they adapt in AI-augmented contexts?

- Recall a time when something was legal but not ethical. How did you navigate it?

- How do you manage value conflicts between yourself, clients, and organizations?

Cultural Competence Development

- How has your cultural heritage shaped your assumptions about communication and boundaries?

- How do you now determine whether your approach to coaching is culturally responsive or culturally imposing?

Adaptive Capacity and Systems

- When have you successfully navigated surprise change? What abilities helped?
- What triggers rigidity for you in uncertain situations? What practices could help you stay open?
- How should the coaching profession evolve to serve human flourishing in an AI-augmented world?

Moving Forward

This chapter has explored how to build coaching infrastructure for an uncertain future by cultivating adaptive capacities rather than attempting to forecast specific changes. Marcus's story illustrates the shift from preparing leaders for known scenarios to equipping them with the mindsets and foundations to thrive in whatever situation unfolds.

The infrastructure metaphor makes the point clear. Systems designed only for predictable conditions crack when the ground shifts. Systems designed with flexibility—extra load-bearing capacity, modular design, safety margins—can absorb disruption without losing their purpose. Coaching must do the same.

For coach education, that means fortifying empathic adaptability, ethical reasoning, cultural fluency, and systems thinking. These are the structural elements that will endure when technologies evolve, organizations reorganize, and global conditions change.

Adaptive capacity is not a single event or credential. It is an ongoing practice: strengthening ethical muscles, rehearsing cultural agility, and building presence that holds steady under pressure. We are not preparing coaches merely to survive disruption. We are preparing them to lead humanity through it, with wisdom, integrity, and hope.

The choices we make today, about how we train coaches, what capacities we prioritize, and which values we embed, will define the future of the profession.

Next, in Chapter 11, we turn to the specific skills that will distinguish coaches in an era where the field itself is in flux. What does mastery mean when models are evolving? Which durable skills will anchor coaching as technology accelerates? The architecture we construct now will decide whether the future of coaching advances human flourishing or merely organizational efficiency.

Coaching Futures—The Skills Tomorrow Demands

Victoria Chen, a Chinese–American executive coach, had been practicing for fifteen years when the existential anxiety struck. Founder of a boutique firm specializing in tech executives, she prided herself on staying ahead of the curve. But after a particularly draining client session, she found herself wondering whether her hard-won expertise was on the verge of obsolescence.

Her client, a senior AI researcher at a major technology company, had filled the entire session with questions she couldn't easily answer: How do you coach someone whose work involves teaching machines to recognize human emotions? How do you help leaders navigate ethical dilemmas that didn't exist five years ago? How do you support identity development when someone's professional success depends on creating technology that might eventually replicate their own cognitive abilities?

Shaken, Victoria called a longtime colleague, Dr. Rashid Patel, a former business-school classmate who had left consulting to pursue research in human–AI interaction. With identifying details removed, Victoria consulted Rashid about the broader ethical dilemmas her clients were raising.

"I feel like I'm trying to coach clients through challenges I don't understand myself," she admitted during their video call. "This client is grappling with ethical questions about emotional AI that I've never encountered. He's managing global teams where some members have never worked with humans and others have never worked with AI. He's trying to keep relationships authentic when half his interactions are mediated by algorithms."

Rashid considered her words carefully. "What if not grasping is where you begin, rather than where you stop?"

Victoria frowned. "What are you saying?"

"You think you need to be an expert in AI research in order to coach him. But he doesn't need another technical expert. He needs someone who can guide him through the human complexity that comes when technology collides with identity, connection, and values."

"But how can I guide him through a country I've never traveled to?" she asked.

"Think differently. You don't need to share his technical knowledge. What you do know is how to help people clarify what success means to them. You know how to help someone analyze their values when facing new ethical dilemmas. You know how to help them preserve real relationships under pressure. Those are not diminished by strange circumstances; they are amplified."

In the weeks that followed, Victoria shifted her approach. Instead of chasing mastery of every new technology her clients mentioned, she focused on fortifying the human development skills that remain relevant in any technological setting. She crafted questions that invited clients to explore their values under new conditions. She practiced holding space for ambiguity without rushing to solutions. She attuned more deeply to cultural dynamics on global teams, noticing patterns she had previously overlooked.

When she met her AI-researcher client again a month later, the conversation was different. Rather than offering advice on designing ethical AI, she guided him in clarifying what integrity meant in his role. Instead of dictating how to lead a global team, she helped him explore how his own communication style shaped team dynamics.

"I don't need you to understand the technical aspects of my work," he said at the close of their session. "I need you to help me understand the human aspects of myself. That's what no algorithm can do."

Victoria realized she had been trying to compete with AI, rather than embracing the fact that her greatest value lay in capabilities machines cannot replicate. Her expertise wasn't in technology; it was in understanding how human beings navigate change, build relationships, and maintain authenticity under pressure.

* * *

Victoria's experience illustrates the fundamental challenge facing coaches as artificial intelligence reshapes professional contexts faster than traditional training can accommodate. The human infrastructure of the AI age requires coaches who can provide stability through adaptive capability rather than static knowledge.

Like bridge engineers who design structures that can flex with wind and earthquakes without losing their essential function, coaches must develop capabilities that remain valuable even as the technological landscape shifts beneath them. The infrastructure metaphor reminds us that durability comes not from rigidity, but from building adaptive capacity into the foundational design.

In a world where both human potential and artificial intelligence are rapidly advancing, coaching cannot remain stagnant. Coaches of tomorrow won't just need sharper questions or deeper empathy. They'll need **future fluency**: the ability to anticipate change, navigate ambiguity, and evolve with purpose.

1. Future Fluency: Reading Signals, Not Just Situations

Today's coaches are trained to observe what is happening in the present. Tomorrow's clients need coaches who can:

- Spot early indicators of disruption
- Distill uncertainty into insight
- See beyond trends to patterns
- Hold space for identity shifts during transformation

This is not prediction. It is preparedness, cultivating the infrastructure of discernment that holds steady when the future feels wobbly.

2. Tech-Awareness Without Tech-Worship

Tomorrow's coach doesn't need to code, but they must understand how technology shapes human experience. They should grasp:

- How AI bias impacts people and power
- The ethics of data privacy and consent culture
- How technology influences attention, identity, and emotion
- The limits of automation in human work

As Dr. Rumman Chowdhury reminds us, "Bias is not just a glitch; it's a reflection of the system that built the model."

Similarly, Harvard Business School lecturer Jeff Bussgang argues that empathy is not a distraction from technological innovation; it's the grounding wire that keeps it human. "Translating AI advances into consumer value," he writes, "relies on human strengths—creativity, empathy, and intuition."

This underscores a truth coaches know intimately: empathy isn't just an ethical responsibility. It's a strategic advantage.

3. Intercultural Intelligence as the Norm

One-size-fits-all coaching models are over. The future belongs to coaches who can:

- Decode global communication cues
- Navigate across race, gender, power, and language
- Translate emotional intelligence into cultural fluency
- Help clients lead in diverse, distributed environments

This isn't a niche. It is the core of leadership.

4. Coaching Systems, Not Just Individuals

More than ever, coaches are asked to influence organizations, not just people. That requires the capacity to:

- Understand system dynamics
- Map power loops and cultural levers
- Support change across policies, not just people

To do this effectively, coaches must embrace humility. We are guides, not engineers. Systems shift through dialogue, not imposition.

5. Radical Presence in a Distracted World

When algorithms automate decisions and distractions multiply, presence becomes a competitive advantage. Tomorrow's most trusted coaches will embody:

- Slowness in a world of speed
- Listening in a world of alerts
- Stillness in a world of optimization

This is not softness. It is a strategy. Radical presence was first introduced earlier in this book as an antidote to scaling pressures. Here, it becomes the anchor for future readiness, the relational infrastructure that technology cannot simulate.

Coaching the Human Side of Change

In times of disruption, people don't just need tools. They need guidance. They need mirrors, not dashboards. Coaches are those mirrors.

Futurist Sinead Bovell warns that the next generation is already forming emotional attachments to AI. Young people may struggle to distinguish between genuine human connection and algorithmic responsiveness. Coaches must help clients preserve the capacity for authentic relationships in environments where artificial empathy grows increasingly convincing.

The infrastructure challenge is building relational capacity strong enough to coexist with AI's convenience without surrendering humanity. Coaches offer what AI cannot: genuine care, cultural understanding, ethical reasoning, and the ability to hold complexity without rushing to resolution.

Illustrative Example

An international executive is tasked with leading AI integration across a global team. The coaching approach chosen will determine whether the effort succeeds or fractures.

Scenario 1: AI-Only Approach

Approach: The coach emphasizes individual development through standard models: goal setting, communication, stress reduction. Ethical concerns are referred to HR or legal, and cultural resistance is addressed with generic diversity training.

Results: The executive develops useful personal skills but struggles with systemic and cultural challenges. Tensions persist, and ethical dilemmas remain unresolved. The scaffolding holds for a time but collapses under new pressures.

Scenario 2: AI + Culturally Responsive Coaching

Approach: The coach integrates the five future-ready skills as a unified framework. They practice future fluency by helping the executive anticipate shifting team dynamics. They apply tech-awareness without tech-worship to contextualize AI challenges. Using intercultural intelligence, they guide culturally specific change strategies. They apply systemic coaching to influence policies as well as individuals. Finally, they model radical presence to sustain trust through disruption.

Results: The executive builds adaptive capacity that endures beyond the project. Cultural tensions ease, ethical reasoning strengthens, and leadership presence deepens. The infrastructure proves resilient, bending without breaking under the strain of change.

Architectural View:

Scenario 1 = temporary scaffolding
Scenario 2 = flexible foundations with long-term structural integrity

Chapter 5 Practice Lab

Activity 1: Assessment of Prospective Skills

- Evaluate your current capacity for each of the five future-ready skills. Identify one strength and one blind spot in each.
- Practice recognizing early indicators of change in your field. Create a plan for coaching clients toward multiple futures instead of a single forecast.

- Research one AI tool relevant to your context. Evaluate it through ethical and cultural lenses, not just technical ones.

Activity 2: Building on Systems Thinking

- Map an organization where you coach. Trace how individual challenges link to team, organizational, and social systems.
- Identify leverage points where personal development could influence broader change.
- Analyze how power, privilege, and access affect outcomes in your coaching relationships.

Activity 3: Infrastructure for Building Presence

- Establish daily routines that preserve attention for deep listening.
- Set explicit boundaries for technology use that protect authentic human interaction.
- Develop discernment strategies to distinguish simulated empathy from genuine empathy.
- Practice helping clients strengthen their own capacity for presence in AI-mediated environments.

Reflection Questions

Future Readiness Assessment

- Which one of the five future skills comes most organically to your current practice, and which one feels most resistant to developing?
- How do you manage current situations when you are not technologically inclined but must support the individual who is undergoing the technology transition?

- What assumptions about coaching practice might need to evolve as AI capabilities continue to advance?

Integration Issues

- How do you balance cultivating new skills with preserving depth in your current strengths?
- When would it be appropriate to refer clients to other professions instead of expanding your scope of practice?
- How do you maintain authentic humanity while integrating technological tools into your coaching approach?

Ethical Considerations

- What is the responsibility of coaches for determining how AI is embedded in human development instead of simply adjusting to whatever tools are developed?
- How would you distinguish between expanding the scope of competence vs. practicing beyond the scope?
- What ethical standards should the practice of coaching follow when working with clients who are designing systems for artificial intelligence?

Systems Impact

- How do individual coaching relationships contribute to broader social change, and what responsibility do coaches have for this impact?
- When coaching challenges reflect systemic inequities, how do you balance individual support with advocacy for structural change?
- What role should coaches play in ensuring AI development serves human flourishing rather than merely organizational efficiency?

Professional Evolution

- How will you further develop these future skills with proficiency in traditional coaching competencies?
- What support systems and learning communities are required for lifelong management of professional development?
- How do you want to contribute to the evolution of the coaching profession as AI integration accelerates?

Moving Forward

This chapter has explored the five core capabilities that will distinguish exceptional coaches in the AI era: future fluency, tech-awareness without tech-worship, intercultural intelligence, systemic coaching, and radical presence. Each of these is powerful on its own. But their true strength lies in their cohesion. Like beams, foundations, and joints in a building, these skills interlock to form an infrastructure strong enough to carry the weight of rapid change.

Victoria's story shows what this looks like in practice. She did not abandon her existing expertise, nor did she try to become an AI specialist. Instead, she integrated these capacities in a way that gave her clients stability amid uncertainty. That integration is the task ahead for the profession.

The infrastructure metaphor reminds us that future-ready coaching must be designed, not improvised. Architects do not build skyscrapers by guessing at tomorrow's weather; they design with flexibility and safety margins that allow the structure to hold under stress. In the same way, coaching education must design for the unpredictable, embedding adaptability, ethics, and cultural responsiveness into its very foundations.

And just as cities require coordinated upgrades to their infrastructure—bridges reinforced, transit systems modernized, water lines expanded—

so too the coaching profession requires collective investment. These skills cannot be left to chance or to individual preference; they must become part of our shared scaffolding, supporting coaches across cultures, industries, and generations.

Crucially, this is not a one-time construction project. Infrastructure requires ongoing maintenance. Roads must be resurfaced. Bridges must be inspected. Systems must be recalibrated. In the same way, coaches must return again and again to the five capacities, practicing, reflecting, and strengthening them over time. The durability of the profession will depend not on one round of training, but on a culture of continual renewal.

We are not preparing coaches merely to withstand disruption. We are preparing them to lead humanity through it, with wisdom, integrity, and hope. These five capabilities are the blueprints for that leadership. But the blueprints alone are not enough. They must be built, tested, and maintained in the daily practice of coaching.

The next and final chapter brings this journey full circle. It weaves together the frameworks, principles, and practices explored throughout this book into a comprehensive vision for coaching's role in shaping humane technological integration. And it returns to the question that has guided us from the beginning: What does it mean to lead with empathy when AI is everywhere? The answer is not found in choosing between human wisdom and artificial intelligence, but in building the infrastructure where both can serve human flourishing together.

Where AI Meets Empathy™

We've arrived at the threshold.

Not of the end, but of the next beginning.

Artificial intelligence is no longer an experiment. It is infrastructure. It is embedded in our calendars, our emails, our feedback systems, and increasingly, in how we reflect, decide, and lead.

But machines are not making us more human. That's still our responsibility.

And that's where coaching comes in.

Coaching Is the Human Infrastructure of the AI Era

Throughout this book, we've explored what it means to:

- Coach with, not against, the machine
- Prioritize presence over performance
- Make cultural responsiveness non-negotiable
- Use data without dehumanizing
- Lead with empathy in an age of automation

These are not goals for the future. They are imperatives, now.

The revolution we've seen across sectors bears this out. Healthcare systems that employ AI for diagnosis still need human clinicians who will convey bad news with kindness. Financial institutions that employ algorithmic trading still need executives who will keep team morale high when the markets are turbulent. Educational platforms that employ machine learning still need instructors who will know when the student needs reassurance rather than yet another practice exercise.

Coaching is no longer a "nice to have." It is the mirror, the map, and the moral compass of organizations navigating a future they can't fully predict.

When the algorithm offers a plan, but the leader feels stuck: that's a coaching moment. When the data is clean, but the story is missing, that's a coaching moment. When efficiency is high, but belonging is low: that's a coaching moment.

Such moments proliferate as integration with AI becomes greater. Every automated conclusion has ripple effects that need human interpretation. Every gain in efficiency becomes a concern for potential losses. Every advance in technology brings forth new ethical challenges better addressed by wisdom rather than intelligence.

Illustrative Example:
Coaching as Compass and Mirror

In one ICI coaching initiative, a senior director implemented an AI analytics platform to enhance team performance. But shortly after, engagement dropped. Trust eroded. People felt unseen.

Through coaching, she discovered what the dashboards missed: fear. Her team felt observed, not supported.

Together, the coach and client reframed the narrative. They co-designed new team rituals to create transparency, autonomy, and care. The client shared, "I stopped asking what the tool could do. I started asking what my people needed. That changed everything."

This is the essence of Where AI Meets Empathy™, when insight is not extracted from people but co-created with them.

Empathy Is the Competitive Advantage

The leaders who thrive will not be the ones with the most tools.

They'll be the ones with the most self-awareness. The ones who can listen across differences. The ones who can translate complexity into clarity. Those who are fluent in humanity, not just in code.

Empathy is no longer soft. It is the skill that keeps systems human. It is the signal that makes leadership worth following. It is the bridge between disruption and trust.

The ICI Commitment

At the Institute for Coaching Innovation, we believe that coaching is the most human technology we have. And we are committed to developing coaches and leaders who:

- Understand systems and shape them with care
- Use AI ethically and design reflectively
- Coach the whole person, not just the output
- Cultivate emotional intelligence and identity-centered trust

This work is not neutral. And neither are we.

We have learned through working with leaders on six continents that quickness in the face of change too often means contributing to the perpetuation of current injustices by default. Today's algorithms codify decades of historical prejudice. Today's efficiency improvements often mean the loss of human livelihoods and social cohesion. Today's innovation often ignores the needs of the most vulnerable.

Our model is built on a simple but transformational idea:

> **When AI meets empathy, coaching doesn't lose power. It becomes the most powerful tool in the room.**

Your Turn

This book is an invitation, not a prescription.

It's your call to:

- Rethink your relationship with technology
- Recommit to your role as a guide, not a fixer
- Redefine what leadership requires
- Remind yourself that your presence matters more than ever

The invitation extends beyond individual practice to collective responsibility. The coaching profession stands at a crossroads where our choices will influence how millions of people experience technological change over the coming decades. We can choose to be passive adapters to whatever AI systems are built, or we can become active shapers of how those systems serve human development.

Each coaching conversation you have, each leader you develop, each organization you influence becomes part of the infrastructure that either humanizes or dehumanizes our technological future. The frameworks you use, the questions you ask, and the values you model all contribute to the collective answer our society gives to the question of what role humans should play in an AI-driven world.

Since machines are becoming intelligent, the most potent thing that we ourselves can do is to be increasingly human.

This doesn't mean rejecting technological advancement or retreating into pre-digital approaches. It means insisting that human wisdom guides artificial intelligence rather than being replaced by it. It means ensuring that efficiency serves empathy rather than eliminating it. It means building technological infrastructure that amplifies our humanity rather than diminishing it.

Let this not be a conclusion. Let it be a beginning.

The beginning of coaching practice that sees AI as a partner rather than a threat. The beginning of leadership development that prepares people for collaboration with machines while preserving what makes us irreplaceably human. The beginning of organizational change that leverages technological capability in service of deeper connection, stronger communities, and more equitable outcomes.

Welcome to the next era of coaching. Welcome to Where AI Meets Empathy™.

The future is not something that will happen to us. It is something that we will create through the choices that we make, the relationships that we forge, and the infrastructure that we shape today. We coaches have the ability as well as the obligation to make sure the future works for human flourishing. We are ready. The tools are here. There is only one question left: will we choose to put them to use in the service of human flourishing?

Glossary of Terms

This glossary provides definitions for key terms used throughout the manuscript, ensuring shared understanding across coaching, leadership, and AI contexts.

AI (Artificial Intelligence): The simulation of human intelligence processes by computer systems, including learning, reasoning, and self-correction.

Accountability: In the context of AI ethics, the expectation that the organizations developing or deploying AI systems are responsible for their decisions and outcomes.

Active listening: A communication technique used in coaching where the listener focuses intently on understanding the speaker's message, both verbally and non-verbally.

Bias: Systematically favoring or disfavoring certain individuals or groups in ways that are unfair or discriminatory, whether intentionally or unintentionally.

Coach: A professional who partners with clients in a thought-provoking and creative process that inspires them to maximize their personal and professional potential.

Coaching culture: An organizational environment that values and normalizes coaching as a key people development approach.

Coaching presence: Being fully conscious and creating spontaneous relationships with clients, employing a style that is open, flexible, grounded, and confident.

Cultural competence: The ability to understand, appreciate and interact with people from cultures or belief systems different from one's own.

DEI (diversity, equity, and inclusion): A conceptual framework that promotes the fair treatment and full participation of all people, especially in the workplace, including populations who have historically been underrepresented or subject to discrimination.

Emotional intelligence (EI or EQ): The capacity to be aware of, control, and express one's emotions, and to handle interpersonal relationships judiciously and empathetically.

Empathy: The ability to sense other people's emotions and imagine what they might be thinking or feeling.

Ethics: Moral principles that govern behavior, actions, and choices, particularly (in this book) as they relate to AI development and deployment.

Fairness: Ensuring impartiality and non-discrimination in AI systems and their outcomes.

ICI (Institute for Coaching Innovation): An organization founded by Dr. Towanna Burrous to prepare leaders and coaches to navigate the technological changes reshaping the world of work.

Machine learning: An application of AI that enables systems to learn and improve from experience without being explicitly programmed.

Natural language processing (NLP): The application of computational techniques to the analysis and synthesis of natural language and speech, used in AI systems that interpret or generate human language.

Powerful questioning: An inquiry approach used in coaching to evoke insight, clarity, creativity, and action.

Self-awareness: Conscious knowledge of one's own character, feelings, motives, and desires. A key component of emotional intelligence.

Self-regulation: The ability to monitor and control one's behavior, emotions, or thoughts, and adapt to changing circumstances. A facet of emotional intelligence.

Social skills: Facilitating interaction and communication with others; a key component of emotional intelligence.

Technostress: Negative psychological link between people and the introduction of new technologies.

Transparency: In AI ethics, the principle that AI systems should be explainable and their decision-making processes open to inspection.

Virtual coaching: A form of coaching delivered through online communication tools rather than face-to-face.

AI + Coaching Use Cases

All AI use cases are optional and must be guided by consent, confidentiality, and coach-led interpretation.

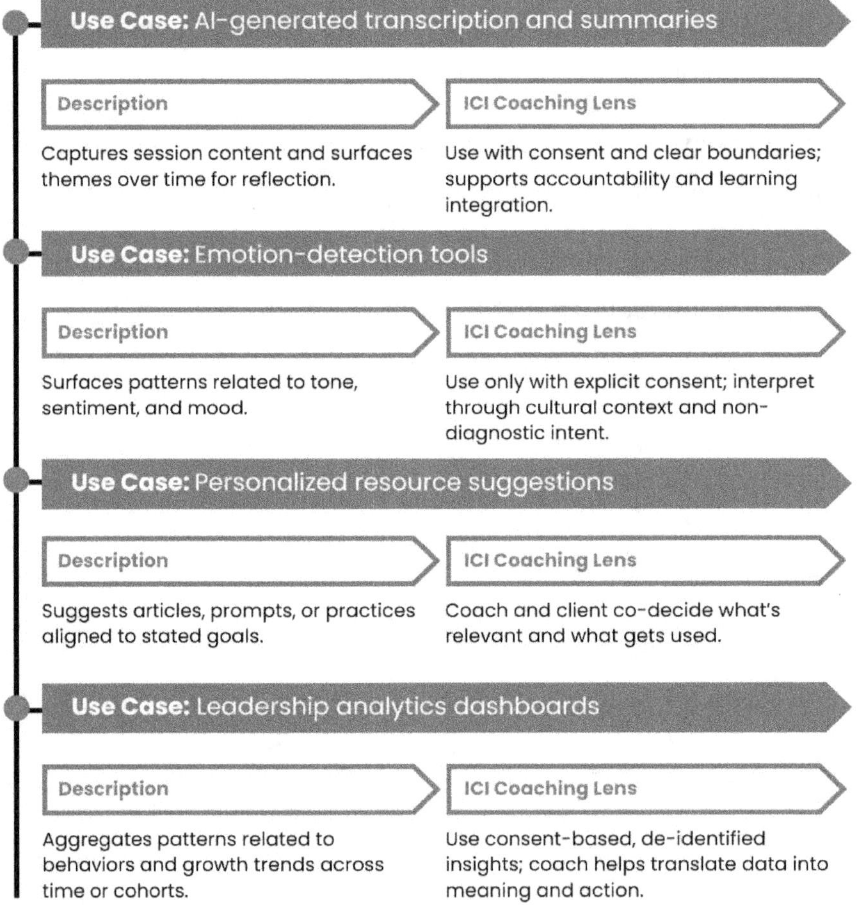

Recommended Tools for AI-Augmented Coaching

Tool: Otter.ai or Fireflies

Function	Notes
Captures session content and surfaces themes over time for reflection.	Use with consent and clear boundaries; supports accountability and learning integration.

Tool: Parabol or Notion AI

Function	Notes
Surfaces patterns related to tone, sentiment, and mood.	Use only with explicit consent; interpret through cultural context and non-diagnostic intent.

Tool: Replai or Grammarly

Function	Notes
Suggests articles, prompts, or practices aligned to stated goals.	Coach and client co-decide what's relevant and what gets used.

Tool: Leadership analytics dashboards

Function	Notes
Aggregates patterns related to behaviors and growth trends across time or cohorts.	Use consent-based, de-identified insights; coach helps translate data into meaning and action.

Tool: Inner.ai or Emoshape

Function	Notes
Emotion recognition	Consider cultural and privacy implications. Use only with explicit consent; interpret through cultural and privacy-aware lenses.

Sample Ethical Consent Template for AI-Enhanced Coaching

Client Consent for AI Tools in Coaching

The coaching process may include the use of AI tools (e.g., transcription, sentiment analysis, learning platforms) to support my goals and enhance the coaching experience. I am aware of:

The specific tools being used

The data being collected and where it is stored

My right to opt out at any time

My coach has explained how these tools are used, and I give consent to proceed.

Signature: _________________________________

Date: _________________________________

Further Reading and Resources

Lee, K.-F., and Qiufan, C. (2021). AI 2041: Ten Visions for Our Future. Currency.

Einzig, H. (2017). The Future of Coaching: Vision, Leadership, and Responsibility in a Transforming World. Routledge.

Lazarus, R. S. (1991). Emotion and Adaptation. Oxford University Press.

Harvard Business Review. (2023–2025). *AI + Leadership Collection.* https://hbr.org/

World Economic Forum. (2023). *The Future of Jobs Report 2023.* https://www.weforum.org/reports/the-future-of-jobs-report-2023/

Stanford HAI. (2023). *White Papers.* https://hai.stanford.edu

International Coaching Federation (ICF). (2023). *2023 ICF Global Coaching Study: Executive Summary.* https://coachingfederation.org/research/global-coaching-study

Bovell, S. (2025, May 6). *Futurist Sinead Bovell warns against kids' growing dependence on AI in education.* The Economic Times. https://economictimes.indiatimes.com/magazines/panache/futurist-sinead-bovell-warns-against-kids-growing-dependence-on-ai-in-education-we-missed-the-smartphone-era-lets-not-miss-this/articleshow/120936793.cms

Chowdhury, R. (2021). *On the limits of fairness: A critical review of fairness audits in AI systems*. AI Now Institute. https://ainowinstitute.org/publication/fairness-audits-ai-systems

Chaudhri, I., and Bongiorno, B. (2023). *The Humane Vision: Designing technology for human connection*. Humane.ai. https://hu.ma.ne

References

This appendix includes core citations from the *Where AI Meets Empathy™* manuscript, white paper, and integrated research base that inform ICI's coaching philosophy, ethical AI integration, and leadership development approach.

* * *

Ajzen, I. (1991). The theory of planned behavior. *Organizational Behavior and Human Decision Processes, 50*(2), 179–211.

Beun, R. J., et al. (2017). Talk and tools: The best of both worlds in mobile user interfaces for e-coaching. *Personal and Ubiquitous Computing, 21*(4), 661–674.

Burrous, T. C. (2021). *A comparison study on e-coaching and face-to-face coaching* (Doctoral dissertation, University of Pennsylvania).

Deloitte Digital. (2023). Ensuring a human-centered approach to AI. Retrieved from https://www.deloittedigital.com

Ertiö, T., Eriksson, T., Rowan, W., and McCarthy, S. (2024). The role of digital leaders' emotional intelligence in mitigating employee technostress. *Business Horizons, 67*(4), 399–409.

Goleman, D. (2005). Emotional intelligence: Why it can matter more than IQ (10th anniversary ed.). Bantam.

Goleman, D., Boyatzis, R., and McKee, A. (2013). *Primal leadership: Unleashing the power of emotional intelligence* (10th Anniversary ed.). Harvard Business Review Press.

Goodman, R. (2018, October 12). Why Amazon's automated hiring tool discriminated against women. American Civil Liberties Union. https://www.aclu.org/news/womens-rights/why-amazons-automated-hiring-tool-discriminated-against

Halliwell, P. R., Mitchell, R. J., and Boyle, B. (2023). Leadership effectiveness through coaching: Authentic and change-oriented leadership. *PLoS One, 18*(12), e0294953.

Hardesty, L. (2018, February 11). Study finds gender and skin-type bias in commercial artificial-intelligence systems. MIT News. https://news.mit.edu/2018/study-finds-gender-skin-type-bias-artificial-intelligence-systems-0212

Houser, K. A. (2019). Can AI solve the diversity problem in the tech industry? Mitigating noise and bias in employment decision-making. Stanford Technology Law Review, 22, 290–354.

Khan, I. (2023). DEI and AI ethics: Striking the right balance. Retrieved from https://iankhan.com

Mayer, H., Yee, L., Chui, M., and Roberts, R. (2025, January 28). Superagency in the workplace: Empowering people to unlock AI's full potential. McKinsey and Company. https://www.mckinsey.com/capabilities/mckinsey-digital/our-insights/superagency-in-the-workplace-empowering-people-to-unlock-ais-full-potential

McKinsey and Company. (2025). The state of AI: How organizations are rewiring to capture value. Retrieved from https://www.mckinsey.com

Nielsen Norman Group. (2023). AI improves employee productivity by 66%. Retrieved from https://www.nngroup.com/articles/ai-tools-productivity-gains/

Passmore, J. (2024). The future of coach education: Adapting to the digital and AI transformation. *Choice Magazine of Professional Coaching.*

Schuller, D., and Schuller, B. W. (2018). The age of artificial emotional intelligence. *Computer, 51*(9), 38–46.

Singla, A., Sukharevsky, A., Yee, L., Chui, M., and Hall, B. (2025). The state of AI: Rewiring organizations to capture value. *McKinsey and Company.*

Van der Pas, D. J., and Aaldering, L. (2020). Gender differences in political media coverage: A meta-analysis. Journal of Communication, 70(1), 114–143. https://doi.org/10.1093/joc/jqz046

World Economic Forum. (2023). *The Future of Jobs Report 2023.* Retrieved from https://www.weforum.org/reports/the-future-of-jobs-report-2023/

International Coaching Federation (ICF). (2023). *2023 ICF Global Coaching Study: Executive Summary.* Retrieved from https://coachingfederation.org/research/global-coaching-study

Additional practitioner insights and anonymized client themes were drawn from ICI-led coaching programs and AI pilot initiatives, 2022–2025, with consent and data ethics protocols aligned to ICF standards.